Praise for *Spiritually, We*

"*Spiritually, We* is a must-read for anyone who feels lonely and disconnected. Sah understands community connection is the basis of our wellness and offers practical and empowering tools to help the shifts necessary to create true happiness in today's changing world."

DR. NICOLE LEPERA
#1 *New York Times* bestselling author of *How to Do the Work*

"Sah D'Simone lovingly shares how the profound power of spiritual connection can heal the pervasive affliction of loneliness in our modern world. With wisdom that transcends the mundane, Sah guides us toward genuine connection, inner harmony, and profound healing."

YUNG PUEBLO
#1 *New York Times* bestselling author of *Inward*, *Clarity & Connection*, and *The Way Forward*

"Sah D'Simone has a powerful gift for making the spiritual liberation path accessible no matter where we are on our journey. In *Spiritually, We*, Sah taps his hospitality gift to beautifully welcome us onto the spiritual path and generously offer us practical insights that help us extend that hospitality to others. I'll be recommending this profound book to everyone in my learning communities!"

CHRISTENA CLEVELAND, PHD
founder of the Center for Justice + Renewal and author of *God Is a Black Woman*

"*Spiritually, We* is a sacred reminder. A salve on an isolated island of invulnerability. Sah D'Simone delivers authentic, real, raw, soul-soothing connection in every chapter and in every space between the lines. This book provides the much-needed Sacred How and Why in a frequently technologically over-plugged-in yet disconnected world. This book delivers an opportunity to crack our hearts wide open in order to remember that we do better . . . *together*."

JENNIFER MULLAN, PSYD
founder of Decolonizing Therapy

"This book is like a warm hug. A gift for any reader and an absolutely necessary conversation regarding healing, community, and togetherness, *Spiritually, We* is a transformative guide that helps us to more deeply understand ourselves among a new global landscape. I would recommend it to anyone who wants to move through life and loneliness with greater confidence, self-love, and ease with this incredibly loving and insightful guide written by Sah, voice of the new generation."

KRISTA WILLIAMS
cofounder of Almost 30 and author of *Modern Tarot*

"Sah is so authentic, full of wisdom, and devoted to serving. Getting to spend time with Sah in any format, whether it be in person, on a video call, or through consuming his incredible work, is a gift that we mustn't take for granted. Thank you, Sah, for turning your journey and all of your experiences and findings into accessibly written wisdom that we all deserve to sit with and learn from."

SASHA AND AJ MARTOFEL
cofounders of Self-Care Is for Everyone

"In a world where crisis is becoming the norm, it is easy for us to shrink into our individual fear and anxiety, forgetting that caring for one another is the path we must choose to bring about a more liberated future. In his characteristically sassy and heartfelt teaching, Sah reminds us that there is no liberation without love, care, and kindness for ourselves and others around us."

LAMA ROD OWENS
author of *The New Saints*

"Reminding us that the work of awakening is communal rather than solitary, Sah offers readers a clear and heartfelt approach to seeing beyond the self in order to walk this path of liberation in community."

SHARON SALZBERG
bestselling author of *Lovingkindness* and *Finding Your Way*

"Sah's voice is a potent reminder that in times where our phones and laptop may seem to keep us more connected, at the heart we are still craving a type of deep, heartfelt, and spiritual connection that is an essential life nutrient. We all need this reminder to not be afraid of vulnerable honest connection."

ALEXANDRA ROXO
bestselling author of *F*ck Like a Goddess* and *Dare to Feel*

"Praise the Goddess for this much-needed book on spirituality and relationship! The invitations, practical applications, and examples, as well as the profoundly deep mystical teachings in this book, will give your heart a soft place to land after encountering the battlefields of modern-day relationships and the all-too-common isolation. Sah's invitation for us to come back together, after thousands of years of living spiritually separate, will tend to the pieces of our broken hearts and create waves of compassion that reach far inside and beyond us as individuals."

ADRIANA RIZZOLO
founder of Body Temple, spiritual mentor, somatic healer, and sex educator

"As a maker of a spiritual community, Sah D'Simone knows well the life-changing impact when we Awaken together. Not all forms of social support are the same. When our deep spiritual lives are shared, we join in care, wisdom, and a world fully inclusive of all souls on earth. Sah points to ways forward to seek a sacred life of deep connection with the Divine and the Divine in each and all of us."

LISA MILLER, PHD
Columbia University professor and author of *The Awakened Brain*

"In this startling new book, Sah's years of contemplative practice and inner truth-telling blend with a gorgeous writing voice and a reverently irreverent sense of humor, lifting him as an essential guide for our times."

MIRABAI STARR
author of *Caravan of No Despair* and *Wild Mercy*

"For anyone who has ever felt lonely, or has longed for a stronger community, Sah D'Simone offers gentle yet powerful guidance toward a more social and supported life in *Spiritually, We*. This is the medicine we all need!"

MO GAWDAT

international bestselling author of *Solve for Happy*

"This is a book about relationships, which begins with giving ourselves permission to be more ourselves. Sah shows us that only from this place can we begin to form and access the deep, vulnerable, and nourishing communities we all crave and need. Vital work for these times."

RUBY WARRINGTON

author of *Sober Curious* and *Women Without Kids*

"Sah is a true spiritual heart—filled with wisdom, compassion, and a whole lot of sass. *Spiritually, We* is a beautiful evolution of his work tackling one of our biggest epidemics—loneliness—from a soul-centered place. I absolutely adore him and this book."

SAHARA ROSE

bestselling author of *Discover Your Dharma* and *Eat Feel Fresh*, host of the *Highest Self Podcast*

"As psychological researchers come to a consensus that we are in the midst of a severe loneliness epidemic, this book is exactly what our culture needs right now! In *Spiritually, We*, Sah lovingly and fiercely beckons us to look up from our navel-gazing and to lock eyes with our community—so that we can experience the rich healing medicine of human togetherness."

SHANNON ALGEO

psychotherapist and acclaimed author of *Trust Your Truth*

Spiritually, We

Also by Sah D'Simone

Spiritually Sassy

5-Minute Daily Meditations

5-Minute Daily Meditations Page-A-Day Calendar

Spiritually, We

The Art of Relating and
Connecting from the Heart

Sah D'Simone

sounds true
BOULDER, COLORADO

Sounds True
Boulder, CO

Published 2024

Cover and book design by Charli Barnes

Printed in Canada

BK06651

Library of Congress Cataloging-in-Publication Data

Names: D'Simone, Sah, author.
Title: Spiritually, we : the art of relating and connecting from the heart / Sah
    D'Simone.
Description: Boulder, CO : Sounds True, 2024. | Includes bibliographical references.
Identifiers: LCCN 2023031652 (print) | LCCN 2023031653 (ebook) |
    ISBN 9781649630797 (hardback) | ISBN 9781649630803 (ebook)
Subjects: LCSH: Spiritual life--Buddhism | Interpersonal relations--Religious aspects-
    -Buddhism | Communities--Religious aspects--Buddhism.
Classification: LCC BQ5400 .D75 2024 (print) | LCC BQ5400
    (ebook) | DDC 294.3/444--dc23/eng/20231128
LC record available at https://lccn.loc.gov/2023031652
LC ebook record available at https://lccn.loc.gov/2023031653

FSC
www.fsc.org
MIX
Paper from
responsible sources
FSC° C000000

In loving memory of my mother

Contents

Introduction

The idea for this book—or, at least, the idea that it was necessary—first started bubbling up for me during the Pandemic. Does that seem too obvious, darling? A book about how critical friendship and community are not just to our physical and mental well-being but also (most importantly) to our spiritual vitality, made clear by the very absence of those things? Yeah, that was sort of how it went, but also? Not really.

I feel a little guilty writing this, but for me, those early days of uncertainty, social distancing, and quarantining brought into sharp relief how damn lucky I am. During the initial storm of the Pandemic, my friendships were shelter, the ultimate safe haven, as my friends and I formed our little bubbles and tried to navigate what the hell was happening to life as we had known it. Confined to close quarters and really faced with the quality of my connections, I could see more clearly than ever just how supportive, healing, nonjudgmental, and full of wild joy my friendships were, how sacred. How they held space for the ongoing work-of-art-in-process that each of us is. And definitely, that might not have come into quite such sharp focus otherwise.

But what was stranger to adjust to was my new *online* reality. For me, the Pandemic meant I had to very suddenly stop traveling. For years, my work—both professionally, as a teacher, and personally, as a student—had been taking me on a near nonstop crisscrossing of the country and the globe, with little rest in between. Now that I was stuck in one place, I had to find new ways of working and connecting with my teachers and students. For the first time, I got deeply into social media and "creating content" (lord, I hate that phrase!). Don't get me wrong. Before the Pandemic, I was in constant contact with other people—but it was largely IRL. I never had a ton of free time, and the last thing I wanted to do was spend what little I did have on my phone. Now here I was, filming myself dancing, making memes, DMing, double tapping, and Instagram stalking (I kid, I kid).

I would be lying if I said that at first I didn't enjoy my new life as a very-online person. It was beyond cool reaching so many people I wouldn't have otherwise, but . . . it was also fucking weird. Over a few months, I started to get more of a bird's-eye view of pop-culture wellness and spirituality, and it wasn't pretty. Okay, it *looked* sort of pretty, and at first I was seduced (I'm always gonna be that bitch, what can I say?): empowerment was the name of the game, and people were up here posting about their villain era, their rock-solid boundaries, the bridges they weren't just burning but blowing up, and all the toxic people in their lives they were done with.

At the same time, I was getting a lot of DMs from folks saying they wished they had friends like me or that they wished I was their best friend. To be clear, they weren't just saying they wished they had a queer, Brown, and fabulously sassy friend (who wouldn't?) or even that they wished they had a close friend or more friends. No. These messages were pretty explicit about how they were on the spiritual path, or at least a therapeutic path, and now their friends just didn't get them. They were so far "beyond" or "above" their hopelessly unenlightened friends, it was a megabummer.

It was about then that I started seriously contemplating writing this book. I applaud the work of getting right with yourself and seeking out other like-minded journeyers. But so many of these videos I was seeing and messages I was getting were operating in a binary world where people are either good or bad, worthy or unworthy, and anyone who fails to meet a standard of moral perfection—a standard that is an illusion—deserves to be tossed away. They had missed the part of personal growth and spirituality where we learn from others, where we exhibit compassion, where you can't "do the work" if you're not working from a place of radical love, both for yourself and others. Healing and freedom aren't about suppressing pain, avoiding difficult people, and shutting out discomfort. And they definitely can't happen all by yourself. But so many people I encounter, online and IRL, seek out only information and relationships that affirm and uphold their personal values and belief systems, even though those systems often go unexamined and even if they are unbalanced or broken. They willingly forfeit relationships with others because it's easier than facing their own blind spots or stepping out of their comfort zones. They build fortresses around themselves that are just as hard to escape as they are to penetrate.

This navel-gazing "me-me-me" approach to healing is some twisted shit, honey. It's *in community* that we actualize the deepest parts of our healing. We all need people. The path to liberation—freedom from our conditioning, freedom from the delusion that we are separate, and freedom to rest in the present with a fresh mind and open heart—*must* be walked hand in hand. Doing the work between you and yourself—that is, your body, your mind, and your heart—is only half of the liberation equation. That's the journey we all know so well: we excavate the depths of our past, we identify and heal our traumas, we feel better. And that's where most of us stop, thinking the work is done. But it's not. The other half of the liberation equation requires doing the work between you and your people and between you and all people—that is, you and your relationships, you and your community, you and every stranger you encounter.

When we stop at the first half of the liberation equation—when we leave behind other people—we leave behind a lot. Growth cannot occur in a vacuum, honey! It's all about our stuff rubbing up against each other and learning from each other. We've got to share ourselves and engage with others because it's only through relationship that the path to full liberation is cultivated. Leaving the work we've done in our heads to benefit only ourselves is a distorted and self-centered expression of the spiritual path, reducing it to a tool for disguised narcissism. The goal isn't just to better your life; it's to better the world. Spirituality should be expansive—it should always be moving from *me* to *we*.

We're in a tough spot. We are all products of and living in a culture rooted in individualism and selfishness, one that denies our personal responsibility to each other and the world. And as my Pandemic-spurred online magical mystery tour showed me—and any quick trip through your socials will show you—even most of the "wellness" and "personal growth" and "spirituality" content circulating through the body of our culture is really about feeling good, "keeping your peace," and avoiding discomfort. Shutting out the world and shutting out other people. The irony is, so much of what we long for in life—whether that longing is for personal well-being, romantic love, fulfilling friendships, meaningful work, or healthier family relationships—is rooted in connecting authentically with other people.

There's a well known story in Buddhism about Ananda, the Buddha's disciple. The story goes that Ananda had a profound insight regarding the importance of friendship in the pursuit of liberation, and was excited to share it with the Buddha. "Teacher, could it be true that half the spiritual path is friendship?" he asked, probably expecting some amount of praise for this radical reflection. It's said that the Buddha responded immediately, "No." Yeah, you read that correctly. No. "Friendship isn't half of the spiritual path. Having good friends is the whole of a spiritual life," the Buddha gently corrected Ananda.

That's what *Spiritually, We* is all about—restoring connection to spirituality and spirituality to connection. It's about the potential for liberation in each of us and how we can realize it through friendships that are sacred: friendships that always reach toward freedom, that remind us of our own constant destiny toward full awakening, that celebrate the miracle of impermanence, and that recognize that we are all artists and that our lives are ongoing, collaborative works of art.

There's no linear path here, my love—this isn't a how-to book— but over the next seven chapters, we'll journey together, exploring the loops and spirals and switchbacks of the liberation equation, figuring out as we go, first, in chapter 1, how we got here, what's at stake, and how we can start making ourselves available for sacred friendship. In chapters 2 and 3, we'll delve deeply into sacred friendship—what it is *not*, as well as what it *is*, so we can avoid the same old friendship patterns we've been trained to think are normal. Knowing what sacred friendship looks and feels like is one thing, but sustaining it is another if we're always checking out or building barricades when things get uncomfy, so in chapter 4, we'll get into why we need to stop avoiding conflict. We'll explore how triggers can be a good thing as well as the difference between healthy boundaries and barbed-wire fences. In chapter 5, we'll get into what lies on the other side of conflict and how to get there with communication strategies for real connection. You can take down your walls, but you still need to get out of your own way for sacred friendship to bloom: in chapter 6, we'll explore one of the biggest obstacles to allowing ourselves to truly connect—shame, and how to move through it. Finally, in chapter 7, with the foundation of all that hard work you've been doing in place, we'll check in with our karma, learning that it takes only a handful of us to commit to becoming sacred friends to heal the entire world. Throughout, we'll explore simple ways that you can be a magnet for friendship and connection in everyday life.

The wisdom and practices that I share in this book are born of my own experience learning to relate to everyone, from my own siblings to strangers on the street and people with whom I've had a difficult history, and are an ongoing part of my own spiritual practice. They come from my heart to yours and will shift your inner state to help you enter the world feeling more "Spiritually, We." Use them as you read the book, and come back to them anytime you have to relate, engage, speak, serve. . . . These are the practices that will help you drop in, fortify, and strengthen or soften yourself before you relate with others. Master these practices, and when you go into the world, you'll strut in with full confidence that you belong in the community. You'll know you showed up in your full power, as your best.

In the course of my own journey (one that is still ongoing) to living my whole wild truth, I have read countless books and attended many workshops, trainings, and meditation retreats, all in an effort to heighten my practice and understanding of myself. I've turned inward, working on my individual healing, focusing on my individual self. And even though that work did bring me to a place where I felt more at peace with myself than I ever had before, it was when I turned my practice outward that I experienced the most radical shifts in my own consciousness.

In my friendships, family, and relationships, I am supported and supportive. With my people, I am celebrated for all my freaky, sassy, wondrous glory. And I welcome everyone in their truth as well. To the people who remain unable to accept me as I am, I send blessings, but I can see that those are not "my people." Not yet, at least. Being able to discern between who belongs in my life and who is just "passing through" is another happy byproduct of my healing journey. I no longer waste my time or energy worrying about impressing people or convincing them to like me. I just show up in my full power and trust that the right people for me will respond.

There is a saying, which is commonly attributed to the Dalai Lama, that "we can live without religion and meditation, but we cannot survive without human affection." If you take one thing away from this book, my intention is that you know you aren't alone, that you aren't meant to be alone, and that it is side by side with others that wisdom flourishes.

Chapter 1

We Need Each Other

First things first. Don't get it twisted, honey: this is not a book about how to make friends. Wait . . . what? Isn't this chapter called "We Need Each Other"? Isn't this book called *Spiritually, WE*? Yes and yes. Look, my darling, making friends is a totally fine subject, sure—especially for a personal development kind of book. But this is not that book. We're not in the realm of "wellness," or even just "growth." No. We are on the high-stakes path of spiritual liberation—and *your freedom is only ever truly actualized in context with the other. That's* the guiding principle of this book.

Okay, I know I just got a little intense. That was fierce af, even for me. But this is serious shit. It's beautiful and joyful, yes, but it's also a wake-up call. I'm sounding the alarm: you can't get free alone. There's no freedom without meaningful connection with other people. We need each other.

The problem is, so many of us have forgotten that. We are living in the midst of a loneliness epidemic, one that is making us sick in our bodies and our souls. Our culture treats "need" like it's a disease when it's really the other way around: our cult of individualism is making us ill and imprisoning us in a world of delusions. Once we can start acknowledging just how much we need each other? Baby, then we're on the road to freedom, on the path to building *sacred* friendships—friendships founded on the fundamental truth of our inherent goodness—that empower us to live bold lives filled with radical love, for ourselves, for each other, and for the whole damn world.

But just diving into sacred friendship when we have been conditioned for so long by a culture that's all about *me, me, me*, a culture that is ill-equipped to support such a radical shift, is a tall order. After all, how do we get well in a sick society where more people than ever live alone, where connecting virtually is the new normal, and where we have fewer and fewer chances to share our authentic selves with another person? As Jiddu Krishnamurti, one of the twentieth century's greatest thinkers on the subject of our shared humanity, reportedly said, "It is no measure of health to be well-adjusted to a profoundly sick society."

We start by unadjusting. And we do *that* by beginning where we are, in the present moment, with ourselves—through confronting our loneliness, practicing radical friendliness, learning to see in the dark, embracing paradox, and accepting the flow of karma (the fate we inherit and the destiny we make as a result of our actions) through our lives. Only then can we make ourselves available for sacred friendship.

Are you ready, my darling? Take my hand. Let's go—together.

The Loneliness Epidemic

It's time to talk about the L-word—loneliness. The emotion that holds so much shame. Why? Because, my darling, didn't you get the memo? You're supposed to know how to self-soothe; you should be able to take care of yourself; you should be okay on your own. Asking for help or using the four-letter word *need* is an admission of failure. I can't even count how many times I've heard someone declare, while talking about their partner, "I want them, but I don't need them," as if this were a badge of honor. "I need help," "I need you," "I need someone." Eeew. What are you, insecure? Codependent?

Is it really so wrong to need others? (Personally, I think our disgust with "need" stems more from a fear of vulnerability than anything else, but hold tight—more on that later.) Maybe you're remembering past relationships—these could be with friends, family, or coworkers, not only romantic partners—where you or the other person was, in fact, codependent. That is not what I'm talking about. Codependency is a *dysfunctional* form of need in which a person is excessively reliant—psychologically, emotionally, or both—on another person for support. This person enables the other's self-destructive behavior, be it a product of addiction, immaturity, poor mental health, or other challenges. Typically, the enabler neglects their own needs and doesn't enforce healthy boundaries. It's all about needing someone at the expense of your own needs. I want to be clear that this is not the kind of needing I'm talking about here.

When I say "need," I am referring to a natural dynamic into which we are all born. At birth, we are helpless. We need our caregivers to sustain us. We are born into a family, and from our first moments, we are in relationship—with our primary caregivers, be they our parent or parents or guardian, with our siblings, if we have them, perhaps with extended family and chosen family. That family exists within a community. As we grow, we more actively join that community. We go to school, we join the workforce, perhaps we are part of a church, mosque, synagogue, or other spiritual community. We establish friendships, we seek relationship, companionship, and friendship at every stage of life, not because we are codependent, but because we are driven biologically to be in relationship, to need others as part of our survival as humans. Being in relationship and in community helps us shelter from the storm because it makes us literally healthier, because it's an ongoing practice that teaches us how to get better at it, because connection to each other and thus to something bigger than ourselves not only feels good but also creates good, and because if we ever want to be truly free, we can do so only in its context.

Needing each other is the most natural thing there is. We have got to unlearn the thinking that need equals weakness and reclaim love, affection, and friendship as our birthright. Our lives and our spirits depend on it. But we can't even begin to do so without looking straight at loneliness rather than away from it. There is nothing shameful about loneliness. Think about it as one of your psyche's alarm systems, alerting you that a critical need is going unmet: your need for connection. The groundbreaking work of neuroscientist Dr. John Cacioppo, who, alongside his colleague Gary Berntson, founded the discipline of social neuroscience, found that loneliness is a cue, like hunger, signaling us to act in service to our survival. Chronic loneliness, Dr. Cacioppo's research demonstrated, weakens our immune system and increases the likelihood of an early death by 20 percent.[1] Research has linked social isolation (infrequent contact with others) and loneliness (the feeling of being alone, regardless of frequency of contact with others) to higher risks of a variety of physical and mental conditions: inflammation, high blood pressure, heart disease, obesity, type 2 diabetes, cognitive decline, dementia, Alzheimer's disease, anxiety, depression, and attempted suicide, among others.[2]

We are driven to connect, so when we aren't connecting, we are simply not living in the truth of who we are. It's not surprising then, that in a recent study, people (mostly men) who possessed narcissistic personality traits (antisocial traits that are toxic to relationships) were found to have very high levels of cortisol in their saliva.[3] Overexposure to cortisol and the release of the stress hormones it triggers can disrupt almost all your body's processes. Not only that, but studies also show that chronic high cortisol levels put individuals at greater risk of long-term health problems, particularly cardiovascular events. This is striking to me because it comes back to the heart. Literally, the health of your heart reflects the health of your mind.

Are you starting to map out the thread of loneliness? If we starve ourselves of connection, we suffer. It's that simple.

And yet the bitter truth is, as a society we are lonelier than ever. A 2021 national survey of American adults conducted by the Harvard Graduate School of Education found that 36 percent of all respondents reported feeling "serious loneliness," indicating that in the four weeks prior to the survey, they had felt lonely "frequently" or "almost all of the time"—but that *61 percent of young adults* surveyed reported experiencing serious loneliness.[4] In a 2018 survey of twenty thousand people conducted by the insurance giant Cigna using the widely recognized UCLA Loneliness Scale, two in five people reported that their social relationships weren't meaningful, while Gen Z respondents (between the ages of eighteen and twenty-two) reported the highest rates of loneliness.[5] Additionally, there was a 30 percent increase in suicides in the United States between 2000 and 2016.[6] These statistics are devastating, but in confronting them head-on, we can't deny the real public health crisis that loneliness presents.

Wanting to better understand how loneliness can have such impactful effects on the body, I spoke with Dr. Rachel Wurzman,[7] a neuroscientist and neuroethicist who studies the role of social, relational needs in healing from trauma and addiction. Dr. Wurzman began by explaining that when we experience social pain such as shame, rejection, and isolation—all of which can produce loneliness—our brain processes it as if it were physical pain, using the same pathways. The problem is, as Dr. Wurzman described it, "When you are in physical pain, your body increases certain stress hormones that cause changes physiologically, so that you can fend off injury and limit its damage in the short term. In the short term, then, these stress hormones are protective. But when we're exposed to these hormones long term, like with chronic pain, we develop chronic health conditions." Now, remember: for all intents and purposes, *our brains can't tell the difference between physical pain and social pain.* Let me pass the mic back to Dr. Wurzman so she can drop it: "What's fascinating, then, is that social pain can lead to the same sorts of effects that any form of long-term stress has." In other words, social pain can make us literally sick.

Social pain also has the effect of increasing the sensitivity of the brain's reward system—in other words, it makes us more likely to self-medicate, to seek pain relief. As Dr. Wurzman explained it, the parts of our brain that hijack our physical pain reflexes to process social pain—the anterior cingulate cortex and the medial anterior cingulate cortex—also have inputs into the ventral striatum, the part of the brain that's involved in addiction and stimulus response. So, when we deprive ourselves of social connection, we turn up the sensitivity of the reward system. What does this mean? It means that lonely people—especially those experiencing social isolation, whether as a result of trauma and shame or for other reasons—will respond to addictive behaviors in a much more heightened way than someone who has a healthy social life. One can understand how lonely individuals would be more susceptible to addiction, whether to food, drugs, alcohol, TV, sex, porn, you name it, because of their brain's heightened reward system. Put plainly, loneliness drives addiction and addictive behaviors. Almost twenty-one million Americans have at least one addiction. Drug overdose deaths have more than tripled since 1990. We have a population of people literally starving for connection and turning to unhealthy ways of coping.

As a sober person, I was of course interested in Dr. Wurzman's take on recovery and loneliness. This is what she had to say: "Recovery from addiction seems to involve . . . a reduction of the things that separate [addicts] from other people, which can be guilt and shame. But the other thing that guilt and shame do is separate us from our source. Interactions with community and interactions with a higher power serve somewhat of the same function in the brain." Why would community and interactions with a higher power serve somewhat of the same function in the brain? Because they're both about connection, honey—connection to something greater than ourselves. I mean, that's what we're saying, sis! Spiritual experiences are innately social, and social experiences are innately spiritual. Recovery from addiction, or any healing, for that matter, requires social connection.

Do you hear this, honey? No one needs or deserves to be alone! We are wired to connect, we thrive in connection, we are meant to be in community. We are a social body, an interbeing. I repeat: connection isn't just about getting your needs met, sweetie. *It's about what's best for everyone.*

Let's face it, though . . . society didn't set us up for success here. What we seek—meaningful connection, tightly knit community—and the society we live in are completely incongruent. Here in the United States, there's nothing we love more than "independence." Individualism is practically our religion. We love a maverick. Our national myths are all about self-made men. We've perverted what independence really means, though, and turned it into an all-or-nothing value. Our culture has a very binary perspective—things are so often "either/or" and almost never "and."

When it comes to independence, the binary dictates that our only other option is dependence (shudder!). We've forgotten all about the truth of interdependence and that needing other people doesn't preclude having an independent spirit.

And capitalism requires our buy-in to this value system. Don't get me wrong; we all need to earn a living, and there's nothing wrong with desiring enough income to live a life where meeting your everyday needs isn't an issue. But the rat race that our culture puts us through each day to make ends meet is making us so stressed that we are completely desensitized to our own needs and the needs of others. Numb. We are then totally unable to hear our inner worlds, let alone hear one another, and we are more likely to self-medicate in this state: the good old quick fix of drugs, alcohol, TV, social media, shopping—pick your poison.

Our culture worships money. We love money, and we've internalized the idea that getting it is pretty much a zero-sum game. We make heroes out of billionaires as the rich get richer and the shrinking middle and working classes slip closer to poverty. And even though most wealth is generational (if that's not dependency, what is?), we like to pretend that the wealthy earned their riches through a meritocracy that doesn't exist. Believing it lessens the pain of knowing, deep down, that institutionalized racism, economic inequality, and corporate interests mean the game is rigged. The notion that we all have equal opportunity is simply not true.

It's all connected. Let's face it: our culture is rooted in some flawed values, values that separate us from our common humanity, that are anathema to community, that encourage superficial connection, and that fuel loneliness. Not only are these values making us literally sick, but they're also limiting the possibility for true healing—for our bodies, yes, but also for our souls.

The model that says we don't need each other has failed us. And to it, I say, "No, thank you." Let me be the first to be vulnerable and say I am lonely, I need help, I need love, I need you. In my years seeking and growing into the teacher I am today (still growing!), I have learned to find power in those statements—because they are the truth. We do need each other. Our health and well-being, both bodily and spiritually, are inextricably tied to the health and well-being of those around us as well as to our environment. It is through relationship that the next level of our healing journey happens, that our liberation takes place. The answer to our twinned crises of loneliness and spiritual stagnation lies in moving from *me* back to *we*—back to community, back to authentic connection.

Radical Friendliness

Maybe "authentic connection" sounds a little too jargony to you, or a little too kumbaya, like you're supposed to have a soul-to-soul spark with every person you meet. But what I mean is something simpler: an interaction, a connection, in which two people actually *see* each other and *feel seen* as the unique humans they are in their unstruck goodness, however fleeting that moment is. And it begins with radical friendliness.

I love the word "radical" a little too much, I know. My editor *might* have asked me more than once, "Please, Sah, find another word." Maybe it's because I'm a child of the '80s, but I prefer to think that it's because nothing else captures what I'm going to ask you to do here: unearth the roots of our conventional ways of perceiving so that we can sow the seeds of a new and deeply different way of perceiving ourselves and others. Because that's what "radical" means, quite literally—the word stems from the late-Latin *radicalis*, which means "root." And in its delightful, delicious, and irresistible (at least to me) use as an adjective, it has come to mean that which is profoundly different from an existing method or ideology. So why *radical* friendliness?

Friendship lies at the very heart of *Spiritually, We*, yes, but not friendship as we have come to know it, which is too often transactional and conditional. No. What I'm talking about here is sacred friendship, which begins with and is built upon radical friendliness. What does that mean? Well, when we are able to approach the world from a place of radical friendliness, it means that we are liberated enough—from our conditioning, from our preconceptions, and from the delusion that we are separate—to view all its people with love.

Okay, that's all well and good, you might be thinking, *but I'm only human. I don't like everybody, let alone love them. And why would I want to?* Fair enough. Here's the thing: I'm not asking you to "like" everyone you meet. This isn't about your emotional response to those with whom you cross paths. In fact, it's the opposite. Emotions are always about *you, not about the other person*—they arise from *your* conditioning and meaning making; they are impermanent and fleeting. The love that fuels radical friendliness is *radical love*. Lord, no, not the R-word again (I know we're all thinking it). But look, when we talk about love, we're usually talking about a feeling. Radical love isn't a feeling. It is an acceptance that we are all innately good. What does it mean to be innately good? It means that everybody—every single person—possesses a fundamental nature that is intrinsically pure, and that all sentient beings have an inherent potential for liberation. Everything else—evil, malevolence, wrongdoing—emerges from illusion, delusion, and conditioning. Basic goodness is always there—it does not need to be earned. Humanity does not need to be perfect, to our liking, or without complication to be deserving of love. It is, and therefore, it is loved. You are, and therefore, you are loved. All living beings are enough, just as they are, and worthy of love. When you move through the world guided by radical love, you practice radical friendliness with everyone you encounter.

Meeting people with radical friendliness doesn't mean you "fall in love" with every person you meet on the street; it means you commit to seeing their goodness and not meeting them with judgment, fear, or insecurity. This, my friend, is the basis of *Spiritually, We*: not only that it is possible to love all living beings but that we must. Remember, in the work of spiritual liberation, only 50 percent happens between you and yourself—the other 50 percent happens between you and other people. The "we" mindset is therefore an initiation, an invitation, and a challenge to accept a lifelong, sacred practice of radical love.

Of course, most of us are out of practice, or we're too overwhelmed by where or how to start. That's okay. After all, I said *practice*. And that's all it's ever going to be—practice, not perfection—because the path to liberation isn't linear. It loops, it has switchbacks, it has dead ends, it's always going to be serving you new opportunities to grow, especially as you move in and out of doing the work between you and yourself and doing the work between you and others. That's why I like to start practicing radical friendliness out in the world through *conscious social interactions* with strangers or acquaintances. Practicing radical friendliness with people you're not superintimate with is, frankly, easier than jumping straight into it with close friends, family, or lovers. Our dynamics with those whom we're close to are often more complicated, tangled, complex, and overlaid with our own narratives. Starting with strangers, or at least people you don't know superwell, helps build your "muscle memory" (the heart is a muscle, after all); it helps radical friendliness become second nature.

So, remember how loneliness and social isolation are different? Loneliness is a subjective feeling that is different for everyone. Social isolation is about how much contact you have with other people. Some people might have little contact with others and not feel lonely. Some people might have a ton of contact with others but still feel lonely. I'd argue, actually, that that's most of us. The problem is that overall, the quality of that contact is pretty poor. We might not be socially isolated, but we're not socially integrated. Social integration is actually knowing the name of your mail carrier; it's learning that the barista who makes your matcha latte every morning is a film student; it's asking how your doctor's kid likes living in the big new city they just moved to; it's helping your child make a birthday card for their teacher; it's grabbing a cup of coffee for the front-desk security at your office building. When we are socially integrated, we are connecting with the people around us, even if only for a few moments, in a meaningful way that underscores that their lives are just as real, important, and complex as our own. We are building the muscle of radical friendliness.

Unfortunately, there's a cultural phenomenon in North America that I like to call chronic "Hi how are you fine." It's the rote, mindless, social exchange we use to move along the transactions that comprise a large part of our days. These exchanges are practically unconscious, they're so automatic. I know, I know, we're all "busy." Busyness is like the second pillar of American identity—we must all be productive producers of labor! But taking an extra minute here and there throughout your day to engage consciously, not automatically, is not going to be the difference between hitting that looming deadline or not (scrolling your socials mindfully will, however—but we'll tackle that in a bit).

Practice: Conscious Social Interactions

How do you initiate a conscious social interaction? First, invest in that person's reality. That means remembering that, just like yours, that person's life is full. Just like you, they have goals, dreams, unmet desires, joys and sorrows, triumphs and traumas. They are a real person who has lived a specific life, so try starting with a specific question: "What's your name?" Use it next time you see them. It may seem small, but when we learn a person's name, we're less likely to reduce them just to their "role" in our lives. Over time, conscious social interactions build connection.

Asking someone how they are should be treated like the sacred question it is. But it's also a hard question to answer. Being specific— "Did you survive the morning rush?"—invites a specific answer, a way out of the fine and busy. It's an implicit way of asking someone "How are you?" while acknowledging the texture and context of the moment. We're not always in a headspace to engage in a meaningful way, of course. Sometimes we're not feeling well, or we are preoccupied, or we really are in a rush. You know what? Just don't ask, then. The point is to be intentional. We should never ask "How are you?" without actively wanting to know the answer and without being ready for a real answer. You can still have a *conscious* social interaction at those times— say hello, make eye contact, express a sincere thank-you. Be heart led in the present moment.

When you ask, "How are you?" and mean it, you change the culture, starting with yourself—you are actively helping to dismantle the pretending, loneliness, and isolation of life as we know it. Conscious social interactions deepen our social integration and help us practice our radical friendliness. Practice walking through the world as a radical friend: meet people in the moment, without narratives about who they are. This means don't assume you know who a person is or what they're going through based on external markers, such as their job, their appearance, or their relationship status.

Remember that every person you encounter is dealing with real-life stuff, for good or ill, whether that's a sick parent, a struggle to pay rent, or the birth of a long-awaited child—and that you have no way of knowing. Remind yourself of what you do know: that they are innately good and that you are not the star of everyone's reality.

Knowing you're not the star of the show isn't just about having a healthy ego—it's about keeping in mind that how other people treat you is rarely personal. Even when we approach the world with radical friendliness, we may not be met with it—and that's okay. Because when we think about radical friendliness as meeting others with love—remembering that they are innately good—we're also saying that radical friendliness is about *making space for people as they are now*. And when we make space for others, we also make space for ourselves. In a literal sense, when we drop our stories and preconceptions about other people, we make space in our minds; we reduce the mental clutter. But we also make a different kind of space for ourselves when we accept others as worthy of love as they are now—a space of grace. When we practice radical friendliness, when we repeatedly connect with the truth of others' fundamental goodness, when we remember that all people are worthy of love just as they are, it cannot escape us that *we* are part of the "all." The more we practice extending radical love to others, the more we come to see that we deserve it, too. Bumping up against the bare, unvarnished reality of this can help soften the stringency with which we tend to treat ourselves. In doing so, we create room for sanctuary within ourselves. And here's the thing: we need space if we want to invite others in.

Practicing radical friendliness is so powerful because it helps us begin to clear our minds of negative thoughts and false narratives that did not originate from our truth—that people are innately good—and that prevent us from engaging with ourselves and others in the honest and vulnerable way that sacred friendship requires. The more we make space for others, accepting that they are enough just as they are, the more we make space to accept ourselves. In this way, radical friendliness allows us to finally open the door to our inner sanctuary—it's not *completely* blocked anymore by the unopened packages, old winter coats, and spare parts of our psychological debris.

Learning to See in the Dark

The problem is, most of us don't want to invite people in—whether we are aware of it or not—because we don't have that uncluttered inner space, that inner sanctuary. Nope, our inner homes are a freaking disaster, and we actively avoid taking the time to clean them up. "Avoidance" is the key word here, honey. Broken friendships we haven't repaired, unchecked behaviors we don't or won't confront in ourselves, misplaced values, lifestyles that are incongruent with what we purport to believe, loss, pain, regrets, shame, fear—everything we want to avoid or don't want to look at, we've stuffed into the closets of our psyche, thrown into the junk room, shoved under the bed, pushed into a corner. It's messy; it's crowded; it smells like old pizza boxes, coffee grounds, mildew, stale cigarette smoke, and something unidentifiable but sour—maybe the wine someone spilled on your carpet the last time you tried to have a party? The stain is still there. There are all kinds of nasty things happening around this inner house. There is no sanctuary to be found. In other words, your house is disgusting to you, you're ashamed, and there is definitely no way you're inviting anyone over, let alone letting them inside. So, overwhelmed and afraid to see the mess, you switch off the lights and leave it to fester. You grow afraid of the dark and what it harbors.

So no matter how much we practice radical friendliness, we won't have enough room within ourselves, or feel secure enough with ourselves, to invite others in unless we also work on cleaning up the mess in order to connect in that deeper way. Cleaning up begins with turning on the lights. You can't know what to keep and what to throw away if you can't see it, after all. You can't even find your way around the house. And no one wants to be stumbling around in the dark and break an ankle. Turning on the lights is tricky, though. Maybe they're burned out from years of neglect. Maybe the power's been cut. They might work—but flipping the switch could be blinding; we've all experienced the disorientation and loss of vision when we emerge suddenly from shadows into sunlight. The hardest part of turning on the lights, though, is the fear of what we might see. It might seem counterintuitive, but in order to turn on the lights, first we've got to learn to see in the dark.

When we choose to clean up our homes, then, we have to choose first to integrate our darkness, to accept it rather than punish ourselves—or others—for having it. People do all kinds of crappy, unskillful, destructive things in the world because they're operating in reaction to their darkness; they're disoriented by the chaos inside them and act accordingly.

What does it mean to integrate your darkness? It means learning to sit with it—learning to just be with difficult or uncomfortable feelings. Our eyes adapt to darkness—think about when you first go to bed at night: initially, the room seems pitch black, but gradually, moment by moment, your eyes recalibrate. The shadowy shape looming off to the side resolves into a bathrobe hanging on the back of the door. The indistinct objects scattered on your bedside table become separate entities again—a book, a phone, a box of tissues. As a child, you may have been afraid of that bathrobe, convinced it was the bogeyman coming for you. But as an adult, you know it's just a matter of perception. Our minds can work the same way. When you are unafraid of the darkness and can be with it, your mind recalibrates. The hard part is being willing to sit with it.

It's easier to sit with darkness if, before you begin, you remind yourself that your mind *will* play tricks on you—it will mistake feelings for stories. Prepare yourself for that. That old shoelace strewn on the floor will look like a snake. Your mind will instantly show you all the times you've been bitten by a snake and all the ways in which a snake could bite you in the future. But the reality is, it's not a snake. It's just a shoelace without any inherent meaning. The only meaning it has is that which you assign it. Difficult or uncomfortable feelings are shoelaces, not snakes.

Keeping in mind that feelings have no inherent meaning is critical to integrating your darkness. Yes, some feelings do have an inflammatory texture. Why? When we get hit with a big emotion, we typically process it not for what it is but for what we think it is. Our meaning-making machine kicks in. We create a story. Say you've just gotten off the phone with your parents. They've just let you know they won't be able to attend an event of great significance to you. The feeling of rejection floods your body. You're remembering every time they've let you down in the past, and now you're telling a story—*They don't care about me; I'm not important to them; if they really loved me, they'd be there.* You process the emotion in such a way that it becomes *about you*, and as a result, the feeling of it—the anger, the sadness—seems fixed, definitive, definitional. That painful feeling becomes calcified, stored inside you, taking up space in your inner sanctuary. Instead of letting the feeling move through you and dissipate, you transform it into a story about your worth. That story hurts, and you're afraid of pain. So you push it away into the darkness, But it's just a feeling. It's a shoelace, not a snake.

There is no snake. So often, when we come into contact with a difficult feeling, we want to change it, to solve it, to fix it right away. To make it go away. Because the moment you touch that feeling of, say, sadness, your mind will dredge up all the sadness you've experienced in your life and, in a misguided effort to protect you, invent a whole new fresh set of possibilities about how you might be hurt again. In an instant, you'll be hurtled into the past, then whiplashed into the future. But here's the thing: you are not in the past or in the future. You are always only in the present moment—and you are safe with yourself. Feelings are not here to hurt you. As strange as it sounds, despite how personal they feel, feelings are not personal in that they move through you, but they are not *you*. Again, they do not have inherent meaning. Just because you feel rejected right now does not mean that you are an unworthy person, or even that you would perceive the same action as rejection in the future. Feelings shift, they change, they come and go, they are impermanent and fleeting. They are a passing sensation—so let that sensation unfold and move on, dissipate, as uncomfortable as that may be. *You* will still be there in the wake of the feeling, in your body, safe.

Sitting with hard feelings is not an easy task, and I won't pretend it is. But you wouldn't be reading this book if you didn't have the capacity to do hard things. It's true that eventually, in service to the path of lib-eration, you will have to get to every room in the ramshackle Victorian mansion that is your psyche, to walk the long halls and turn every corner, switching on the lights as you go. And as you stand at the threshold of your inner sanctuary, you might feel overwhelmed at the prospect. That's reasonable. It would be much easier to skip rooms, even entire floors. But the thing is, you don't have to take it all on at once. As with everything, this is ongoing work. But for now? You can (and must) 100 percent learn to see in the dark by starting where you are: in your body.

The place of transformation is in your body. There's no context for healing if you're not in your body. Why? Because it's only in that realm that we're not lost in the future or the past. Where is the body? In the present moment. Where do we feel our feelings? In the present moment. Where does healing happen? In the present moment.

It's kind of crazy to realize how much of our days we spend con-ceptualizing, narrating, locked in mental effort, when the basis of our spiritual path is to be in our bodies. Often, when we're unable to be in our bodies, to tune in to our feelings and the sensations in our bodies, we're not receiving life. We are criticizing life. We are narrating, we're storifying, we're pathologizing. We are rejecting and separating, or worse. As Pema Chödrön says, "The most precious opportunity presents itself when we come to the place where we think we can't handle whatever is happening. . . . Most of us do not take these situations as teachings. We automatically hate them. We run like crazy. We use all kinds of ways to escape—all addictions stem from this moment when we meet our edge and we just can't stand it. We feel we have to soften it, pad it with something, and we become addicted to whatever it is that seems to ease the pain."[8] But when you *are* in your body, when you can stay there, you are able to witness the quickness, the short life span of a feeling. You experience the miracle of impermanence.

Practice: Sitting with Uncomfortable Feelings

When big stories come up in your mind, that's a signal that there are big feelings in your body that need attention. With the practice that follows, the goal is to get comfortable tuning in to those feelings as sensations in your body without attaching any stories to them so that you are able to stay in the present moment. Try this practice the next time you experience a challenging feeling and you're in a place where you can pause and take a few moments out of the flow of your day. Remember, you are safe with yourself. Feelings are not here to hurt you.

First, turn your patient attention to the feeling and welcome it. Tell it (this doesn't have to be out loud), *I welcome you, and I accept you. I accept that in this moment, I feel hurt; I accept that in this moment, I feel hopeless, frustrated.* Whatever it may be.

Now, if it's safe to do so, close your eyes. Take several deep breaths. Send your awareness through your body, into your neck, your shoulders, your torso, your limbs, your hands, your feet. What do you notice as you do so?

You may notice tingling, stiffness; maybe your eyes are dry, your legs feel jittery, your stomach feels jumpy. These are all forms of tension in the body. Where are you feeling it most? In your belly? Your throat? Your shoulders? Bring your awareness to the sensation. Let your awareness touch it.

You might notice your mind jumping in here. "Oh, my God, I'm anxious because . . ." you hear yourself thinking, and then a story begins unfurling. Let the story play out in the background, but don't engage. Keep your awareness on the sensation. This means that instead of bringing a ton of effort to shutting out the story—which would redirect your energy *to* it—loosen your grip; *don't* make an effort. Lightly let the story go; let it wander off and do its thing. Don't waste energy fighting it. A useful mantra here is *Drop the story and deal with the feeling. Drop the story and deal with the feeling. Drop the story and deal with the feeling.*

Return to the sensation. Don't pathologize it. Just touch it with your awareness. Awareness has an innate quality of warmth—think about what it feels like to be *really* seen by someone, to be witnessed with eyes of love. To feel the warmth of their awareness. That's the warmth you need to bring now to the sensation in your body. Touch the sensation with the warmth of your awareness, processing it in the body, letting it break down and dissipate.

As the feeling passes, notice the tension in your body release. This is all about tension. When there's a big feeling in our bodies, we are in a state of contraction. There's tension in the body; there's tension in the mind. If there's tension in the mind, you're not seeing reality clearly. Your vision is distorted by the tension. Now, notice how upon releasing the tension, your body goes from contracted to relaxed, to a state of expansion.

This state of expansion helps you to see reality in a different way because your vision is no longer distorted. This means that if you are willing to stay with a feeling, you can come out the other side with the ability to see others differently (this is especially helpful in moments of conflict). It means that you can see experiences differently. You can see that a feeling is just a feeling and that the meaning that accompanies it is something you supply, not a truth the feeling reveals.

With practice, dropping into your body like this can be especially revelatory when you're transitioning between environments, like from your car to the parking lot, from the train to the platform, or from the sidewalk to your office—you get the idea. Often, as we cross from one place to another, we experience a lot of fleeting emotions—and thus bodily sensations—that move so quickly, we barely register them. Tuning in to your body at these times can help underscore and clarify the transient nature of feelings.

As you get more comfortable with this practice, I encourage you to try it, as appropriate, when you find yourself in moments of tension with others. Each sensation that you can bring awareness to, without associating an entire narrative with it, switches on the light in another room. This is the path into your full awakening.

Every time we witness the miracle of impermanence, we are closer to liberation. In sitting with our feelings and dropping our stories, it becomes more possible to shed a binary perspective and to understand that things are neither good nor bad; they just are. Our conditioning lifts and we are closer to nonduality, to the understanding that we don't exist in opposition to each other or separately from one another.

When you learn to see in the dark, you realize that you don't need to be afraid of what lives in the neglected or avoided corners of your mind. Your perception can adjust to darkness, empowering you to turn on the lights so you can start figuring out what to let go of. You are free, even for just a moment, from binary ways of thinking and have entered the territory of nondualism, where you understand that all of existence is interconnected; you can see that whatever you've stored away is just an aspect of your psyche, neither good nor bad, and that how you relate to it, even trauma, is relative to how liberated you are. I am *not* saying that horrific events or circumstances do not occur or that we are not devastated by them—I am saying that the more we can integrate our darkness, the more we can learn to see in the dark, the less *suffering* there is in painful experiences.

In modern spirituality and wellness culture (which likes to dress up as spirituality), there's this emphasis on "love and light." It's like a parody of itself now, an Instagram meme, a plaque you can buy at Target, right? I just know you're seeing that hand-lettered script in your mind's eye. But it's not love and light—it's light *and* darkness, you know? The thing is, because our inner light is so much harder to find than ever, we seek desperately outside ourselves for whatever can bring lightness. We're so hungry to be in contact with the sun that we have lost sight of the fact that half our life is lived in moonlight. We're conditioned to reject darkness, and yet darkness is essential to our well-being. Night is a time of rest, of restoration, of intimacy—there is a gentleness to it. And night itself is full of life, of vitality. In Los Angeles, where I live, jasmine flowers scent the darkness. The marine layer rolls in and cools the city, bringing with it the saline tang of the ocean. Coyotes run along the spine of the hills, owls send out their echoing calls, and mountain lions emerge to hunt—reminding us all of their drive toward life, toward wildness, even in the midst of the city. The darkness is full of life. When we can hold that truth in our mind, we can begin to embrace the essential paradox of being human—that life is almost always serving us an "and" rather than an "or." When we fail to embrace this, we fail to embrace life in its fullness—which, of course, means *people* in their fullness.

Embracing Paradox

So you've been practicing radical friendliness, you've cleaned up your inner sanctuary (or at least you're cleaning it—it's an ongoing process), and you're ready to start inviting people in. You're feeling ready for sacred friendship. And then you remember—or are forced to remember—that there are just some people you find, well . . . annoying. Yeah, you're trying to make space for other people as they are now, but it's one thing when that person is a stranger on a rush-hour train and another when it's your actual flatmate, and they're sitting in your inner sanctuary getting crumbs all over your new Togo sofa. No matter how much work you've done on yourself, when your stuff is rubbing up against someone else's, their behavior may trigger an unhealthy dynamic, an old way of behaving, or an automatic response. Hey, growth doesn't happen in a vacuum! With some people, you might know what's likely to set you off, but with others, especially as you build new connections, it can be hard to predict. The only preparation you can really do is to welcome discomfort.

Welcoming discomfort is all about embracing a mindset of paradox. All those difficult people in your life you can't avoid? Coworkers, family members, classmates, friends of friends? These relationships demand a mindset of paradox—the willingness to see people as not just this *or* that but this *and* that, opening ourselves up to being surprised, even delighted by them. People are contradictory; they can be selfish *and* kind, small-minded *and* generous, extroverted *and* insecure. Our minds don't like contradiction; it's not comfortable trying to hold two seemingly opposing truths in mind simultaneously. We want things to be neat, orderly, categorizable, because it helps us make sense of the world—and allows us to stay comfortable and self-righteous. But when we label people in these one-dimensional ways—"He's a slob"; "They're hopeless";

"She's superficial"—we are in a place of limiting judgments, and we've already lost the plot.

Paradox, on the other hand, challenges our beliefs, makes it hard to slot people into categories, and requires us to consider whether our judgments might just be . . . wrong. It's not comfy being wrong. Paradox also offers us a way out of the binary mindset that is so ingrained in us, a way past "right and wrong." It allows us to change our minds—not just reconsidering an opinion or belief but literally changing how we perceive.

Let's look at an example. Let's say my cubiclemate, Sandy, is unbelievably grating to me. She complains all day. She talks constantly about the most obnoxious things, things I just don't care about. She asks inappropriate questions. In my view, she is abrasive and unlikable. But if I open up to a mindset of paradox, I can broaden my view of Sandy. Sandy has good parts as well as annoying parts. She volunteers at an animal shelter—she pins photos to her cubicle walls of herself and the cutest dogs. She is a talented baker—every holiday season, she brings the most delicious homemade cookies to share with the office. Sandy also has parts that you don't know. You don't know what her childhood was like, if she's ever been in love, if this job was what she imagined for herself. Even when (especially when) Sandy starts to be demanding and annoying, unkind, or impolite, if for one moment, you are able to see that she is speaking from her hurt, from her pain, from the part of her that's at war with herself, you've initiated the mindset of paradox. When you do so, when you can hold all of these truths in mind about Sandy, the way you see her, and thus the way you respond to her, will change.

With difficult people, this ability to change your mind is often your only option, because changing your environment is not an option. You can't just quit your job because your cubiclemate rubs you the wrong way. And if you did? I can guarantee you that wherever you land next, there will be another Sandy. We can't live in a state of constant avoidance; we can't just get rid of people, run away from them, or shut them up.

Where does our power lie? In changing our minds. In embracing paradox and inhabiting a place of potential and openness. And it's there, my friend, in that place, that a karmic momentum of radical possibility exists.

The consequence of opening up to a mindset of paradox (Sandy is annoying *and also* sweet) is freedom: the power to choose. I choose to see Sandy as unkind *and also* generous. Sandy is aggressive *but also* gentle. There are three realities: the reality of what I see, the point of view from the other person's experience, and the spiritual potential of what I don't know, what I call "the third truth." When I embody nondualism, I open up to the third truth. There's good, there's bad, and there's *what is*. This is the third truth. Good, bad, *and* something else. It's all about making room for the *something else*, and not just making room but even finding delight in the great surprise that is life.

The binary mindset, on the other hand, is not only disempowering but also takes you into a spiral of negative and false thinking. One annoying comment has the power to take over your day and your mental space. Is it worth it? All it takes is Sandy commenting, "You're late again," and your mind races to, "I can't fucking stand her." Which triggers, "I hate this job." Which prompts, "This job is terrible, and I only have it because I can't get a better one. Which sets off, I'm such a fuckup." Cue all the reasons you're a fuckup. Here, you lose all of your power and become a victim. When you embrace paradox instead, you open yourself to "parts vocabulary" (both this *and* that can exist simultaneously) and learn to see yourself as made up of different parts, too—and that you are a whole greater than the sum of your parts. When you do this, you stop allowing your insecurities to comprise your point of view. You stop allowing everyday interactions to trigger confusion, anger, and insecurity.

When we change our minds, we set in motion a chain of events not visible to the eyes; we initiate a certain magic. When we invite paradox, we are working with mystical energy. You don't have to have a conversation with Sandy and say, "I am choosing to see you in a more expansive paradoxical view" (that would be weird and condescending). You just need to change your energy, to empower yourself—every time you see Sandy—to see her for more than her annoying parts. They are just parts. It is imperative that *every time* you encounter someone who irritates or frustrates you, you recognize that those behaviors don't tell the whole story of that person. In that split second when your mind remembers that "there is more going on here than I can immediately see," you set in motion a new way of being, and you sow positive karmic seeds. While we can never know the exact effects of karmically beneficial action, your ability to see good will invite more good to you. You will become a magnet for positivity and positive change. Slowly, you'll notice that you're surrounded by more positive people, and more opportunities will arise to change your circumstances for the better. It starts with meeting people in an embrace of paradox.

It is possible to love complicated people, to love people who make mistakes, just as you hopefully love yourself despite your imperfections. Similarly, it is possible to be in spaces that challenge you; otherwise, how will you grow? We've got to start embracing the fullness of life and stop hiding from it. One of the ways we hide is by attempting to exist in a bubble. Don't get me wrong; we should aim to curate a life that is joyful, filled with friends we love and whose company we enjoy—that's why you're reading this book!

But the unavoidable reality is that none of us get to live in a bubble (though a lot of us try). We can't go through life without experiencing anger—nor should we want to. Existing in your full humanity means experiencing your full range of emotions. I'm not suggesting that you give people with toxic behaviors more time than you have to or stay in unhealthy relationships—but I am suggesting that extending love to people you're not crazy about is critical to being in the world as a person capable of sacred friendship.

Next time you're "setting a boundary," cutting a person out of your life, or calling out to cancel someone and then posting triumphant memes about self-care on your Instagram stories, ask yourself, "Am I really taking care of myself, or am I engaging in the wellness equivalent of spiritual bypassing?" Remember, it is in the everyday, in community, that wisdom is brought from the theoretical realm to lived experience. There are spiritual lessons in the most mundane of activities, behaviors, thoughts, and feelings. Those times we're faced with difficult people and circumstances that trigger us? Those are opportunities to grow, to practice strengthening our ability to embrace paradox, one of our most critical tools for building sacred friendship.

The Flow of Karma

There's a difference, of course, between everyday annoyance (or even burning-hot *I-can't-stand-you* vibes) and deep, long-standing hurt. Embracing a mindset of paradox is significantly harder when we're dealing with people who have caused, aided, or abetted trauma we've experienced. The thing is—and this won't be pleasant to hear—it is not only possible but critical to extend love, radical love, to everyone in our lives, even the most difficult of all (them *most of all*). Why? Because living in a state of blame and victimhood doesn't get us anywhere. It keeps us stuck, in fact—stuck in the past and stuck in the dualistic delusion of separation from one another.

The problem with this is the past is moot. It happened; it can't be undone or relitigated. When we live in the past, we are living in opposition to life itself, which takes place in the present. When we argue with the past (about what could have or should have or would have happened, if only), we are arguing with reality. When we resist reality, we cannot access the present moment—accepting reality is critical in participating in the present moment, which is the only reality there is. Freedom is only possible in the present, the only place we can truly inhabit. It's as simple as this: you cannot be present when you are in the past.

Extending radical love to those who have hurt us does not mean pretending that our pain does not exist, excusing the actions of others, or diminishing personal responsibility. It means accepting reality, accepting that what happened happened, and loosening our grip on our stories *about* what happened (ascribing fixed meaning and narratives to events), especially when those stories cause shame.

One of the best ways to both make the practice of acceptance less difficult (because, darling, it's *hard*) and "rewrite" the stories we tell about others in relation to ourselves is to first understand and make peace with the flow of karma. In Buddhism and Hinduism, karma is like a law of nature in which a person's actions, for good or ill, over time generate far-reaching consequences in this life and the next. Karma is with you at birth. In the Buddhist view, there's no concept of original innocence in which we come into life with a blank slate. In this framework, what you experience is the product or effect of accumulated actions, not just from your current life but also from past lives. This doesn't mean you deserve anything bad that happens to you—not at all. It means that you have the power, the will, the freedom to disrupt the course of that karma by learning its lesson—and to create a different future for generations to come after you.

Maybe the law of consequences makes sense to you, but past lives just don't resonate with your belief system. Think of karma as generational wounds transmitted through your family tree. Researchers in epigenetics, the study of how environment affects gene expression, have begun to find that the effects of trauma may be passed intergenerationally—that while an experience such as famine cannot "rewrite" a gene, it can affect whether it is "turned off" or "on" and that those "instructions" can be passed on from parent to child.[9] The implications of this research suggest, just like karma, that experiences that predate you can absolutely be a part of you—part of your inclinations, habits, behaviors, and personality. Our stories don't begin at birth; some parts of our makeup are generational wounds that predate us, that are passed down to us.

Of course, we all have stories we tell ourselves about our lives. We know the plot by heart, and while we might not be sure yet who the hero is (hint: it's you), we definitely know the villains. And in our stories, the villain's toxic behavior is always deeply personal. How could it not be? It's our story. It's about us. Villains have their own story, too, though—and yep, their story is about them (hint: they're probably not the villain in their own story), not you. And so it goes, back over time. Each of us is focused backward, on the past, on who did what to whom. The paradox is that this narrative chain is both kind of right and totally wrong. It's wrong in that other people's behavior is rarely ever personal—it isn't about us, actually; it's almost always about their own history, their own conditioning, their own patterns . . . their own karma. Their behavior is not a response to us but an orientation to life (you know, hurt people hurt people). And this type of narrative is kind of right in that it hints at that fundamental truth: *it didn't start with us.* You, me, our parents, society as a whole—we are all subconsciously recreating traumas that have passed to us through previous generations. This is complex, layered, and, I know, heavy shit. But, don't worry, I got you, boo—you're learning a radical, spiritual way of shifting your perspective and disrupting these patterns.

When it comes to the karma of it all, think of it this way: each of us arrives with a backlog of karma, *and* each of us lives in the present moment of karmic possibility, in which we understand that we live in a world where everything comes to be because of something else; everything is interdependent (nondualism). In the now karma, our lives are governed by the law of consequence, where anything said, done, thought, felt, or spoken has either a beneficial or a harmful consequence.

At the same time, our current karmic reality is created by the consequences of our previous actions and the actions of those versions of ourselves from previous lives. Our *future* can change based only on how we respond to what is karmically blooming right in front of us in the nowness. This is what people mean when they talk about karmic lessons—not that karma is a punisher, but that it is a teacher. Every experience offers us an opportunity to reflect, to learn about ourselves and others, to grow.

For many of us, our childhoods caused us an immense amount of pain. They were formative years before we had developed any real coping skills. Our parents, caretakers, teachers, and society *are* responsible for the hurt they caused us, but the ultimate spiritual truth is panoramic and shows us that everyone is profoundly hurt and unconsciously recycling their wounds into the present moment, repeating the same mistakes their parents and everyone in their lineage made. Because of their own unhealed trauma, they recreate the chaos with everyone they come in contact with, and sometimes, too often, we are on the receiving end of that.

Understanding that we all show up earthside with a backlog of karma (or intergenerational wounds)—and that, for many different reasons, some of us are better equipped to learn its lessons as they arrive—can help us to unlearn the old hero-and-villain stories we've been telling ourselves through depersonalizing the actions of those who feature in them. It doesn't mean the person isn't responsible for what they did but that they acted out of their unique karma rather than in response to something about you. It also means *you* are not responsible for *their* karma. In other words, it's not your "job" to try to teach others a lesson; your only job is to try to learn the lessons of your unique karma.

Thinking about things from a karmic perspective can make it easier to loosen our grip on blame. Loosening our grip on blame doesn't mean what happened to us didn't happen; it means that we shift our energy from focusing on the past to the present, to disrupting those destructive patterns rather than repeating them. How do we then disrupt the pattern? Through acceptance. Let's be clear: acceptance is not approval. Accepting that someone did something wrong is the ability to recognize that the wrong happened; it doesn't mean that you're giving consent for more of it to happen. When we accept our experiences, we're not saying they should have happened, only that they did. We stop struggling with reality; we stop adding suffering to pain.

Struggling only reinforces those destructive patterns; it is always reactive rather than proactive. When we stop struggling, we step away from our narratives and our need to be right. When we accept, we stop resisting the fact that things are what they are. It *also* means we understand what they are *not*. There's so much suffering that comes just because we resist reality as it is. But if you accept what is, you stop struggling. A sense of okayness follows. The energy you've given to avoiding, evading, arguing, is freed up. Arriving at this place is so rewarding. Allowing the pain from those that hurt us to heal, instead of picking at the wound and letting it fester, literally creates energy for new relationships.

There comes a point in a spiritual path when we have to learn how to be okay with things that are not okay. The fourteenth Dalai Lama said, "True change is within; leave the outside as it is."[10] Not out of complacency and not out of apathy but from the place of having the emotional resilience and skill to manage situations and people that are difficult. To be of this world is to accept that pain and suffering are happening within it and within you, too. It's about acknowledging that bad things happen and that pain is a part of life, but that we don't need to make the pain worse by fighting against it. The path to freedom is not in avoidance of hard things; it's *through* hard things that we develop wisdom. Being okay with *what is* is a skill in itself. It means we are not chasing the next high, whatever that may be for you—sex, alcohol, attention, drugs, food, whatever your poison. Those self-medications, those numbing mechanisms, do not ready us for connection or lead us to freedom.

When you have faced your own pain, you can face the pain in the world, in your friendships, in your community, even in your family. You're equipped to engage with the suffering of other people in a kind, peaceful, and hopeful way. You inspire others to accept their pasts. When it comes to relating to your own heart, you've stopped dwelling in your suffering, you've stopped ruminating. You're kinder to yourself, you're more likely to know when enough is enough. When you're working through acceptance and healing the relationship with yourself, you're better able to then bring the loving, fierce compassion of acceptance into the lives of other people in your community. Remember, it's in community that we can really test our material, test the work we've done internally out in the world. It's one thing to be able to forgive yourself for your mistakes—but does the hard-won understanding that made that possible now translate into an ability to forgive others for their mistakes? When you test your material in relationship and realize that you're still glitching, still wobbly, that's a sign that your inner world—the relationship between you and your mind, body, and heart—still needs work. That's the liberation equation at work. Living this equation is a dance that requires you to choreograph some moves and at the same time just go with the flow, following the drumbeat of your heart.

Practice: Acceptance

So much of what gets in the way of acceptance are our *attitudes* toward it, which are shaped by our culture's toxic attitudes toward "strength" and "weakness." Perversely, acceptance can be seen as relinquishing some kind of honorable "battle." Because those attitudes can be so pervasive, so ingrained, they can be hard to recognize in ourselves. So when you're feeling resistance to accepting the reality of difficult events, past or present, close your eyes and try reciting any or all of these statements that resonate with you:

- *I am not weak; it takes strength to face a painful reality.*
- *I am not giving up; I am choosing to stop draining my energy into the past.*
- *I am not surrendering; I am letting go of what has never been mine to control.*
- *I am not passive; I am actively alive in the present.*
- *I am not giving a free pass; I am focused on my own karma.*

Once you're feeling less resistance within yourself to the very idea of acceptance, you can try reciting any or all of these statements that resonate with you as a more direct practice of acceptance itself:

- *I accept that there is pain in this world, and within me, too.*
- *I accept that what happened happened.*
- *I accept reality as it is.*

Chapter 2

Sacred Friendship

Friendship is a strange beast. More than just a social need, a matter of safety in numbers that we've adopted over the generations, it is also a biological imperative that heals us at the cellular level. In her book *Friendship: The Evolution, Biology, and Extraordinary Power of Life's Fundamental Bond*, science writer Lydia Denworth challenges the notion commonly held among social scientists and anthropologists that friendship is "purely cultural, an invention of human society—and modern human society at that." She charts how *the desire to make friends* is deeply biological, demonstrating how the "social brain," which helps us understand our relationships to other people and mentalize (to recognize other's mental states and how they affect us) begins wiring itself at birth. Friendship is as old as the savannas, she writes—in other words, friendship has been with us from the beginning of our evolution.[1] It's written in our blood, in our bones, in our brains—it is part of what makes us human.

And yet, for so many of us, though we may be surrounded by friends, our friendships are anything but essential. They're anything but *sacred*. They feel fucking complicated. Hard to make, hard to keep. What's up with that?

Look, in theory, our role in relationships is simple—or it should be. It's to be a spiritual gardener. A sacred friend is a spiritual gardener. What does that mean? It means that within yourself, you cultivate the right amount of sunshine, the right amount of water, and the right amount of fertilizer to tend and nourish not only your own karmic garden but the gardens of others. A sacred friend cogardens the seeds of liberation inside you; they actively water the seeds of love, compassion, joy, and wisdom while helping to weed out that which is not in your true nature. A sacred friend is a botanist to your benevolence. It's a reciprocal process—by bringing clarity to the parts of each other that need work, and through giving and receiving nourishment, sacred friends grow and flower together.

Meanwhile, back in reality, many of us suck at gardening. We might be working hard to make ourselves available for sacred friendship, but because we're habituated to toxic ideas about what friendship is, we're mindlessly spraying around pesticides and dumping fertilizer on weeds. Our own misguided actions are sabotaging our ability to make and sustain sacred friendships. We all have the potential to have a green thumb, though—we just have to unearth our embedded ideas about what friendship is and replant the seeds of sacred friendship. In other words, in order to really understand what sacred friendship *is*, we first have to delve into what it *is not*.

Sacred friendship is not a numbers game, it's not transactional, it's not about superficial validation, and it's not about "fixing" people. Those kinds of moves, though? They pretty much define how we operate in regular old friendship on the daily. Deep down, we know how to share, how to bond, how to cohabitate—but we have bought in to a culture that, however much it touts "freedom," is deeply antithetical to true liberation, and our ways of relating, our toxic dynamics, are products of that culture. When it comes to friendships, we get it so wrong: we prioritize quantity over quality, we focus on what others can do for us, we confuse the easy high of "likes" for affirmation of our goodness, and we believe we know how our friends should be living better than they do themselves. But each of these mistakes has an offering for us—once we understand how and why we do these things, we can transform the impulses behind them into strategies for meaningful connection.

It's Not a Numbers Game

Friendship is such a unique phenomenon; unlike so many relationships in our lives, we choose our friends. We are so afraid of being on the outside, though; we so much want to belong, to be part of an in-group, to avoid ever having to be alone with ourselves, that we can be, well, less than discriminating when it comes to whom we choose. Social media, with its emphasis on follower count, only worsens this impulse. (And don't get me started on how grotesque its transformation of "friends" into "followers" is to begin with.) The more the better, right? Wrong.

We might believe we're cultivating a lush, beautiful karmic garden, but the reality is that most of our gardens are overrun with weeds and have unwanted root systems to pull: friendships that are depleting us, enabling harmful behaviors, or reflecting versions of ourselves we have already outgrown. Realistically, a single person can care for a garden of only limited size—that's why the Huntington Gardens here in LA or the Keukenhof in Amsterdam or the Tivoli Gardens outside Rome— just pick any incredible, huge garden you can think of—are manned by crews, not a lone dude with a rake. It's counterintuitive, but many of us need fewer friends. Fewer, *better* friends. Closer friends.

We need to focus on our *inner circle* and be intentional about our relationships. Evolutionary psychologist Robin Dunbar is known for "Dunbar's number," the *maximum* amount of stable relationships an individual can cognitively manage. That number is 150—but it includes *all* your relationships: your family, your lovers, your friends, even your professional relationships. Dunbar visualizes those relationships as a series of four concentric circles, each ring indicating greater intimacy as it moves toward the center. The outer ring, which comprises all 150 people, is the "weddings and funeral" layer—the people who would show up for that once-in-a-lifetime event. The next ring comprises fifty people, the housewarming crew, the big birthday-party bash. The next ring of fifteen represents our core social circle, the people we know well and trust enough to watch our kids in a pinch. The last ring is made up of your core five relationships, the people who will drop everything when you really need them, the people you turn to at times of deepest sorrow and most profound joy, the people who—at least most of the time—make you feel seen for who you are and love you unconditionally. The ones you can call when you're gripped with guilt and regret and remorse, who will listen without judgment. Whose hand you'd want to hold when going through hard times. And for whom you'd do the same. These are the most important relationships of our lives, the ones that will help us live longer and keep us emotionally healthy, supported, and loved.

How do you determine who those people really are? That inner circle should comprise the people you can trust with your deepest self, your insecurities, and your triggers. They know your story and won't manipulate it later to use against you. I like to think of these five people as being those who can hang with you in the plane of secrets—that plane of existence where your mistakes, the ways you've hurt yourself, the ways you've hurt others, can't be hidden. It's the place where you can show up disheveled, feeling horrible, looking crazy, and let down your burdens without fear of judgment or rejection, where your secrets are held safe. These inner-circle five have this capacity because they also want the same things out of life that you do. They likely have their own ways of getting there, but they strive to be compassionate to others; they want to be of benefit to others; they also want to not be the same person today that they were yesterday. They're in touch with impermanence and let its magic work through them. They're disciplined spiritual warriors—they're moving along the path of liberation with you.

They can meet the darkness in you because they have worked on, or they are working on, their capacity to meet the darkness in themselves. They know that they have hurt others and hurt themselves. They have direct contact with the scary aspect of themselves and of life. And that's what dictates a really deep, sacred, core-five thing—it's not that we all have to have done things we're not proud of or that hard things have to have happened to us. No. It's a depth of common humanity, a shared understanding of how fragile life is and how transitory and how, in a sense, we are always in the grief process. They have touched the grief, because even though impermanence is miraculous, it is also an experience of loss. That's the nondual nature of change: it is simultaneously an erasure and a becoming. Our core five can hold us in that nondual perspective.

The trouble is, many of us take those core five for granted. We fill our lives with so many obligations, socially and professionally, or we lose ourselves in the parasocial relationships of online platforms, that we no longer bring focus to our inner circle. When we lose focus, when we scatter our attention across an ever-widening social circle, our relationships are bound to lose depth and our connections become more superficial. We are all living in the reality of limited time; the hours of each day are fixed; we have only so much time to offer others. Likewise, our energy for others is not unlimited, so we have to use it wisely. In speaking about the layers that make up Dunbar's number, Dunbar himself noted, "The layers come about primarily because the time we have for social interaction is not infinite. You have to decide how to invest that time, bearing in mind that the strength of relationships is directly correlated with how much time and effort we give them." In other words, be intentional in your relationships.

Right now, stop and really consider "How intentional am I in my relationships?" What does that mean? Being intentional means that your choices are purposeful and thoughtful, deliberate. They're made with an end goal in mind—in this case, connection.

Practice: Intentional Connection

- Take a piece of paper and fold it in half vertically.

- On the left-hand side, make a list of the five people you spend the most time with outside work.

- On the right-hand side, make a list of the five people you consider your inner circle.

- Do any of the people in your inner circle appear on the list of people with whom you spend the most time? (It's true a lot of us don't live in the same place as our inner circle folks—but the idea here is just to get a sense of where your energy goes.)

- For each person on the left who is not in your inner circle, write down which Dunbar ring you would actually place them in.

- Now, for every person you've written down, answer the following questions:

  - Do we invest roughly the same amount of effort in our relationship?

  - Do I leave this person's company energized or drained?

  - Do we bring out the best in each other, or is our relationship based in negativity, like mutual complaining?

  - Is the quality of our connection natural—is it easy to be together, or is it stilted, awkward?

  - Does this relationship feel like an obligation?

  - How much do I trust this person?

- Reflect on your answers and consider how well they align with how much time and energy you give each person, especially considering which Dunbar ring you placed them in. Ask yourself, "Am I nurturing the right relationships?"

It's Not Transactional

Be intentional in your relationships, absolutely, but also enter into relationships with the intent to be a sacred friend, and operate with a purity of intention. What does that mean? It means that your behavior in relationship should be driven, as much as possible, by the desire to connect. When you bring bullshit, bullshit follows. It's that simple. Your intentions must be pure. Unfortunately, in our culture, friendship has become increasingly transactional. The foundations of many of our friendships are based on how we can directly benefit one another: "What can this person do for me?" "How can this person help me?" or "What can I get out of this person?" We may not even be consciously aware of this but still seek out friendships that we subconsciously choose as a means to affirm or elevate our status.

Transactional friendships and the status they could deliver were my lifeblood for a good part of my twenties. I thought I was on top of the world during this time—or at least I thought I should feel that way. When I was about 25, I launched what would become a successful fashion magazine with two friends (who, as it would turn out, were definitely not part of my core five). Our success over the next two years meant I had money for the first time and a lot of new peace that came from that security—I was living the "American dream" after all. In doing what every immigrant kid dreams of doing, building success in the United States, I had thought I would unlock some kind of magical happiness. And yeah, I was living the high life (literally and figuratively—I was high all the time). It was glamorous, honey! But I was just as addicted, depressed, anxious, and chaotic as ever.

Then one day at the office, in the fall of 2012, I overheard my cofounders, my so-called friends, conspiring to buy me out of the company. To push me out completely. As I listened, I could feel my heart pounding wildly in my chest, my breath rushing like the ocean in my ears. My muscles twitched. I felt the walls closing in. I was like a trapped, panicked animal. Despite the fact that it was a miserably cold and wet day, I clambered out onto the fire escape, desperate for fresh air. My body felt paralyzed, but my mind and heart were racing. My skin burned hot with shame, and I chain-smoked in a frenzy, trying to figure out what to do. I couldn't believe what was happening and had no idea how to move forward. Failure and hopelessness washed over me as I stared seven floors down to the steaming New York City alley below.

In a rare moment of clarity, I understood the only way out was down—or through. The universe offered me a moment of grace, and I realized I wasn't ready for down. Walking calmly back into my business partner's office, I looked her in the eyes and said, "Listen, I overheard your entire conversation about how done with me you are. Instead of buying me out in increments, just buy me out now. I'm ready to leave." It felt so good to take the reins for that moment. I had felt out of control for so long, despite my best efforts to trick myself into believing I had it all together, and this act of self-ownership felt like a rebirth.

But the next day, when I woke up and remembered what had happened, I thought, "Who am I now?" Without my prestigious job title and glamorous lifestyle, did I even exist? I spiraled out, hopeless and filled with fear. Forcing myself to get dressed, I skulked back to the office, head down, sunglasses on, too humiliated to look at anyone directly. The tension was palpable. Around me, I could hear people's whispers. I quickly packed up my stuff and slithered out. It was the ultimate walk of shame. And nobody said a word to me. Not even one.

In the following weeks, I tried applying for jobs and reached out to friends for leads on what I could do next. I found myself genuinely shocked that no one was available for me. Where was everyone? This was one of the worst moments of my life so far . . . and I felt utterly alone. I had lost my career, and now it dawned on me that I had lost my friends, too, abandoned by the whole world I had built around myself in New York. It was clear to everyone that I no longer had anything to offer them.

I ran to Florida to be closer to my family (and because, let's be honest . . . I had nowhere else to go). Sitting on the beach one overcast and moody day, staring out at the ocean, it struck me that it was as if all the relationships I had had in New York had never happened. All the friendships, lovers, and colleagues that I had thought were real had just dissolved into nothingness, as insubstantial as mist. Surrounded by the warmth of my family, I found enough distance from that life that I began to be able to mourn it properly. I grieved for all the versions of myself that I had had to invent and then bury, over and over through the years. I grieved for all the parts of myself that I had buried under drugs, ambition, and vanity.

It was around that time that, desperate for relief from my suffering, I started digging into self-help and spiritual resources. My cynicism was laid waste by my abject hunger to be rebuilt. One day, my dad suggested that I read some of the work of the Dalai Lama. This seemed totally random to me, as my dad was definitely not the type to study Buddhism in his leisure time. Part of me was like, "What the fuck do you know?" But he knew. He knew.

One month later, I was on a ten-day silent retreat in the Himalayas. The last three days of the retreat were about meditating on death. In the midst of it all, as I pictured the eventual end of this life, I started to feel profoundly sad about all the lies I had been fed and believed and the lies I had perpetuated. Lies I had told and been told by society, my family, even friends. Looking back on the way I had related to people in New York, I could see then, for the first time, that it had always been transactional. A very selfish power-money mindset. My thoughts were always focused on myself: "What's in it for me?" "What can you do for me?" "How can I use this person to succeed?" I viewed people as disposable, replaceable, a means to an end.

As sad as it is to say, I couldn't think of many times that I had actually been there for people in a genuinely compassionate way. I couldn't remember many people calling me to cry on my shoulder. I couldn't remember many people calling me to help them. Even my "best friends" were intoxicated with their own lives. There had been no true connection. It hit me like a ton of bricks. Of course no one was there for me when I needed help! I was never there for anyone else. Not in an authentic, selfless way, at least. If I ever did something for someone else, it was either to get a leg up or be "owed one." It was honestly supergross. But I really didn't see the habit clearly or understand the impact of those actions until I started my spiritual practice and looked inward for the first time.

The transactional way I had related to people had brought me to one of my worst bottoms, and yet it was totally common and acceptable in the world I had been inhabiting. I don't mean that people were explicitly aware of it or acknowledged it but more that it was par for the course. In reflecting on that time in my life while developing this book, I sought out clinical psychologist Dr. Lisa Miller, the founder of Columbia

University's Spirituality Mind Body Institute—the first Ivy League graduate program and research institute in spirituality and psychology—to discuss why this way of relating is so endemic in our society. Dr. Miller noted that we are trained from early childhood to see each other through this transactional lens. We first learn to understand ourselves based on our skill in the school setting. We see ourselves with a fixed mindset ("I am good/bad at this"), rather than a growth mindset ("I can learn how to do this"), in which we identify our "strengths" and "weaknesses": *I'm good at reading but not so good at math; I'm good at sports, but I'm not so strong at writing*, etc. We come to know ourselves and how we can contribute to the world based on our skills and our aptitudes (with the idea that these are innate or fixed rather than something we can work at), even our outward appearance. And we're taught to see others this way, too, in order to draw comparisons between them and ourselves. We pit children against each other. They internalize the idea that learning is not about curiosity and growth but about winning and being better than others—and that there is only so much room at the top. Not everyone can be an "A" student. We are not taught our intrinsic worthiness and goodness but rather that some are better than others and that if we work the hardest, we can be the best.

This has left us as a culture with a toxic rating system for determining the value of one another. When we set foot in a room, it begins: who has value, who doesn't, who is worthy? We evaluate people almost instantaneously, based on almost subconscious cues, before we even begin speaking with them. Once we do begin speaking, we often engage in a subtle form of status interrogation: "What do you do?" (Meaning, of course, what do you do for work?) Maybe, depending on your age, it's "Where did you go to school?" In a sense, we are assessing what the other person has to exchange or trade with us that will further our own goals, be that career progression, social elevation, etc. We desperately need to flip this system. Our default needs to be that we are all already worthy of love, with nothing to prove, no skills to exhibit, no conditions. Forget about your talents, your skill set, your earning potential—all of that is irrelevant in terms of your worthiness.

You are enough already, and so is every person you encounter. We all hold unlimited potential in our vessels. We are all channels for all the wisdom in the universe, with the capacity to light up the world. Our job, when we set foot in a room, is to gift the people in it with love, to see them as souls on earth, and to exult in the delight of everyone as pure potential for love.

Practice: The Blessing Factory

When it comes to seeing people as souls on earth and exulting in their potential for love, one really important practice that I rely on and use frequently is the blessing factory. I use this when I'm not present, when I'm ruminating, when my mind is looping on something, when I have a thousand tabs open in my mind, and *especially* when I'm judging people—when I'm slipping back into that transactional mentality, sizing up what people are "worth."

- Offer everyone a blessing (to be clear, I definitely mean silently)—that might sound like *May you be happy, may you be happy, may you be happy, may you be happy, may you be happy.* Or *May all your dreams come true, may all your dreams come true, may all your dreams come true.*

When you can make this offering, it can bring you back to the present moment in an incredibly powerful way. You'll notice immediately that though you may have judgements going on in the background, they aren't dominating. You become a spiritual gardener and immediately sprinkle around the seeds you want to grow while weeding out those you don't.

Another way we subject each other to transactional thinking is by demanding complete reciprocity in friendship. "Reciprocity" is such a buzzword in conversations around relationship, yet so often it's really a covert symptom of greed, of hoarding and holding on, that will always inevitably lead to suffering. Yes, harmony and fairness should be present in sacred friendship, but sometimes you give more than you receive, and other times you receive more than you give. Sacred friendship is not about a perfect balance. Sacred friendship exists in the material world, where *nothing* is always fair, always in balance. That's not reality, so seeking it will not bring you happiness and peace.

Sacred friendship transcends the ways of the usual human world, and operates on spiritual laws. It is important to remember as a sacred friend that when you give something to someone, you may not get anything in return from them. You may experience karma in the form of a message from a total stranger. My friend Violet told me of a time when she paid for a friend's rent, not expecting anything in return. A week later, while grocery shopping, a thought passed through her mind: "I wonder if Diya is ever going to get her shit together and pay me back?"

A few moments later, Violet was hit unexpectedly with a traumatic memory, one that sent her into a spiral of guilt and shame. A psychosomatic response flooded her body: she felt like the walls were caving in on her; she felt completely cold; her vision blurred. Rushing from the store, she left everything behind in her supermarket cart and stumbled to her car. While in her car, she was overcome with emotion and overwhelmed by suicidal ideation. It had been more than three years since that had happened to her, three years in which she had worked, with her therapists, doctors, and spiritual practices, to keep herself safe.

As Violet sat there, terrorized by her own mind, a stranger knocked on her window. Violet rolled down the window; the person asked her, "You okay?" Violet answered, "Yes, I'm fine," though this was the furthest thing from the truth. The stranger looked at her for a moment and said, "Just so you know, you can let go of your past," then walked away. Violet was so shaken that she couldn't even say thank you. She tried to look for the person, but they were gone.

In her mind, she realized, this was the universe coming to her aid at a moment of extreme distress, just as she had come to Diya's aid by paying her rent during a critical time of need.

What we do for the one we do for *everyone*, for the greater good. When you water a tree in the forest, you are watering the entire ecosystem.

When I nourish you, it is going into the nutritional food bank for all of life. What blesses one blesses all. The feedback, the reciprocity, the payment doesn't always come in kind, but it always comes, if we look for it.

It's Not about Seeking Validation

Superficial friendships and friendships that we treat as transactional naturally breed confusion when it comes to what authentic validation is—what it looks like, feels like, sounds like. Focusing on how many people "like" us and what they can give us is ultimately a search for confirmation of our own value as a person, of our worthiness—in other words, it is validation seeking. But this type of validation, which is rooted in how others perceive us because of what we have, can never be a conduit for true connection because it doesn't actually reflect who we are.

Validation is a tricky subject, especially when it comes to relationships. We all have a subconscious need to hear "Hey, you're moving in the right direction; keep going" or "That's wrong; time to course correct." We're all hoping for that loving mirror that will reflect what we're doing right and what we are doing wrong. We all have a drive to know our goodness, to know, really know, that we are inherently worthy of love.

There is nothing wrong with this need; it's what I would call enlightened or authentic validation seeking. It *does* matter that those with whom we're closest, be it a friend, a parent, a lover, or a mentor, validate our fundamental worthiness. When they do, when they offer us enlightened, authentic validation, we experience deep connection. We hear, feel, and see our goodness reflected back to us. If they don't or can't, they're not in a place where they can hold space for sacred friendship—they're not available to be that botanist to our benevolence, our goodness. Ultimately, though, enlightened, authentic validation has to come mostly from within: it is something you offer to yourself, an acceptance and approval of who you are, as you are. It's owning your fundamental worthiness.

For most of us, our primary source of validation is not ourselves, though—it's others. Things get sticky and tricky here, not only because we're not secure with ourselves but also because we totally misunderstand what *should* secure the approval of others. This is the shadow side of validation. The things we think make us worthy? That's where we get it wrong. We seek validation (both internally and externally) through so many avenues that will never lead us to the truth of our innate goodness and worthiness: through good grades, people pleasing, our appearance, the signs of status we gather around us, our jobs, cars, homes. Our colonized, indoctrinated minds mistake stuff, the worldly, the material, which is inherently flawed, for a direct correlation with or direct mirror of someone's innate benevolence, innate goodness.

But the validation you get from what you have, what you look like, what you drive, where you live, where you went to school, will never really be enough; it is a counterfeit of happiness only masquerading as the real deal, because it doesn't come from within (it's oriented toward the approval of others) and because, in our future-tripping, status-obsessed, more-more-more culture, the goalposts are always moving. A few years ago, one of my close friends quit her high-status job just after she turned forty. I was a little surprised, because her identity and her work had always seemed very entwined to me—and she definitely didn't strike me as vulnerable to a "midlife crisis." She had always been a supergrounded human, seemingly in touch with her values and doing her best to live by them. A couple of weeks after she left her job, we went for a hike, and as the calm of just being in our bodies, out in the noisy "silence" of nature, settled over us, I asked her how she was doing. What she said hit hard.

She told me that even though she thought this so-called milestone birthday wasn't that big a deal to her, as it approached, she found herself ruminating on her own mortality and filled with dread. Lurking in the dread was the fact that she wasn't exactly happy—was, in fact, maybe kind of low-grade permanently sad. "I've been oriented toward achievement my whole life," she told me.

> You know, my parents, their messaging was like, "You have to have good grades, you have to go to a good college, be a doctor, or a lawyer, or a professor, you have to have a high-status job." And I grew up surrounded by people

who believed the same things. So I did all those things. But no matter what I did, I always felt like I could have, should have, done better. I could have gone to an even better college. And then I was ecstatic that I had made my way into this, like, dream career. But then I pretty quickly started to feel like whatever title or rank I achieved in that field, I should have done it earlier. And you know, at every stage, I just felt like I hadn't met some standard. My pride and pleasure in my achievements always faded quickly, and I became focused on what I hadn't done or what I needed to do next. Even so, I felt like it was my work that made people think I was interesting, or cool, or smart. I felt like without it, who would I be, and why would anyone be interested in me?

But around forty, I was like *I've been doing this my whole life, and it hasn't made me happy.* I still don't feel like I've achieved anything. I don't feel like I've met whatever bar I was supposed to meet. And then it hit me: I never will. That bar will always be raised. So what am I doing? Seeking approval externally has never brought me any sense of goodness; it's only made me feel like a continuing failure.

As we talked about the work of discovering how we validate ourselves, it struck me that my beautiful friend's need for approval had been something like an addiction—she had to keep upping the validation ante in order for the next dose of approval to hit the same way. When you're caught in the shadow side of validation seeking, yes, you may just get approval. But that approval is ephemeral and unsustainable. When we rely on it for our self-worth, we become trapped in a cycle much like addiction. Being praised, complimented, noticed feels *so* good. We become addicted to validation, dependent on it to dull the prickling sensations of shame, unworthiness, lovelessness we've developed. It becomes an insatiable need.

One of the most common ways we now find relief for our cravings for validation and approval is through social media. Social media can be a tool for connection, sure, but it can absolutely become toxic, a platform for seeking validation and praise instead of connection. In that way, sadly, it mimics real life quite well. Most of us use our phones and scroll through social media with reckless abandon, no limits at all. How many of you have tried to push your phone away to get work done or even announced that you were "taking a social media break" only to slowly pull the device back into your hands for just one more fix? Is it an addiction? If not, it's something like it. Meanwhile, we're being sold more stuff on our devices and getting our attention and sense of connection from people we either don't actually know in real life or to whom we're showing a very limited, very curated portrait of ourselves (and vice versa). It feels so good to post a picture and see those fire emojis come flowing in or post a political statement and hear that echo chamber tell you how righteous you are, to hit *refresh refresh refresh* every millisecond.

Dr. Wurzman, the neuroscientist who helped us understand the rela tionship between loneliness and addiction, also explained to me that social media activates the striatum, the brain's reward hub. According to her, social media makes us think we're connected when we're really not by stimulating the parts of the brain that are aroused by social rewards. Social media is extremely successful at securing our engagement via highly rewarding stimuli (attractive visuals, short bursts of information, etc.), but it's less intrinsically rewarding than one-to-one social connection that's not mediated by a screen. As she put it, "It's kind of like eating carbs: you eat a piece of Wonder Bread, it tastes delicious, and you feel a little energized from it, but then comes the crash. It's not sustainable. It's not replenishing. It's not nourishing."

The unfortunate truth is that spending time on social media, which is changing and evolving all the time, throws us into a spin cycle of what we need, of what we don't have, of not feeling enough. It reinforces the flawed notion that the more we have, the happier we are. Greed culture depends on our addiction to this kind of validation. When you live by the untruth that the right stuff will make you feel good—the right clothes, the right car, the right education, the right address—all the things you don't have become all the evidence you need, every day, to buy into the lie that you don't belong, aren't good enough. So you buy more, achieve more. But society says you will never have enough; therefore, you'll never be enough. In Buddhism, this kind of cycle is simply called suffering. Suffering is all-encompassing. If you live in a way where what you have dictates your self-worth, then you're always going to be far from experiencing true connection to people.

The simplest way to ease your grip on the need for unenlightened validation is to upgrade your code of ethics. I mean, calling it "simple" isn't really fair, because what I'm talking about is lifelong work—but I don't think what I'm talking about is hard to understand. It's not complicated—in that way, it's simple. If you live by a higher code of ethics, or a higher code of morality, meaning you're consistently kind to other people, you're kind to yourself, you take care of other people, you practice compassion, and if you can't help others, you're at least not hurting them; if you're doing what I would call the basics—if you have this baseline of morality, then your mind is more relaxed because you're not overthinking the things that you did wrong, the things that you didn't do or should have done instead. The need for affirmation of your own worthiness isn't as voracious, because you operate in a state of knowing you've been acting with love and compassion. Once the mind is more relaxed, you have access to the true nature of the mind, which is innately benevolent.

As I said, that's the work of a life. Even while we're doing that work, though, we still need to strive to be in touch with enlightened validation and to do our best to resist the shadow side of validation. The surprise is that the best way to really familiarize yourself with enlightened validation is to offer it to others.

Practice: Affirming the Good in Others

This exercise is focused on *emotional* validation. In other words, it's about expressing acceptance of another person's emotional experience, whether or not you see eye to eye with them (because this is not about you and how you view the world). When you validate someone's feelings, you validate that their *experience* matters. And when you validate that another person's experience matters, you are validating their worth, their value, just as they are—you are affirming their basic goodness. Because we are interdependent and exist only in the context of the other, it can be deeply meaningful to have somebody reinforce that we exist as benevolence itself. In this way, empathetic emotional validation is a powerful form of enlightened, authentic validation.

- First, understand that emotional validation is a process that begins with active *listening*. When someone is expressing their feelings to you, regardless of how challenging those feelings may be, give them your undivided attention and make eye contact. Signal with your body that you are *present* and undistracted. Do not interrupt them.

- Next, when someone is done expressing their feelings, you can *reflect* and *mirror* what they said. Don't try to problem solve, don't offer advice, *do not minimize their feelings* ("I think you might be overreacting"; "Maybe that's not what they meant"), and don't make it about yourself ("That reminds of the time my sister was mad at me because . . ."). Reflecting and mirroring mean demonstrating that you heard and understand them by acknowledging the feeling and the situation: "You have so much on your plate at home; no wonder it feels like your partner is not carrying their share of the load." Notice here that you're not agreeing that the partner isn't carrying their load; you are affirming your friend's feeling, her experience.

- Offer *support* and use validating language—you can say things like "I'm here for you" or "We can talk as long as you need" or "What do you need?" Please, please don't offer platitudes like "Don't worry, it will work out" or "Things always happen for a reason." Phrases like these don't comfort;

rather, they express *our discomfort* with hard feelings and painful situations—they are essentially a way to shut down a conversation when we don't know what to say. Don't know what to say? Acknowledge the difficulty—"That sounds really hard/difficult/painful/frustrating"—don't shy from it.

Affirming the good in others, especially when they are experiencing challenging feelings or expressing an emotional response with which you may not agree, is a powerful way of offering them authentic validation. Doing so is powerful medicine for yourself, too, because it requires a lot of heavy lifting on your part—you have to get out of your own way, you have to connect, and in order to connect, you have to be vulnerable, and that vulnerability has to be honest in order to land.

This is true of offering validation to others in general—such as expressing admiration to another person or complimenting them. When we do it out of pity or as an automatic response, when there is no heart in validation? That's the shadow side of validation, unenlightened validation. True validation means seeing the person for who they are and letting them know they are seen. Our good qualities are who we are; our bad qualities are here to show us who we are not. Unfortunately, we overidentify with them. When we can remind people of the best of themselves in an authentic and meaningful way, we are not only connecting with them, we are helping them connect with the truth of themselves: their fundamental goodness.

It's Not about Fixing People

Accepting people as they are, as we do when we offer authentic validation, is one of the nonnegotiable foundations of sacred friendship. When we enter into sacred friendship or sacred community, we *must* enter the relationship with full acceptance that people are who they are and where they are. And yet the inability to do this is not only one of the greatest but also one of the most common obstacles to building and sustaining deep connections. Almost all of us engage in, have engaged in, or will engage in what I call "Fixer Syndrome": the belief that we can and should fix people and their problems (or the belief that we know what their problems are). Indulging in this misguided idea is one of the most common ways we get in our own way when it comes to sacred friendship. Look, we've all been in that relationship, romantic or platonic, where there's just one little thing (oh, and another . . . and wait, one more) about the other person we wish we could change, whether it's their dirty apartment, lack of ambition, or relentless good cheer (I mean, what a drag). Meanwhile, it goes without saying that we could all use a little fixing ourselves. But the fact is, your bestie or boyfriend or brother may not change as quickly as you would like, or even change at all. And that is, that has to be, okay. Let's get into it.

We tend to engage in Fixer behavior in two different contexts: when there is a problem—and when there's not. Wait, isn't that all of life? Ha. Let's check that dualistic thinking. Awesome. Now, in all seriousness, sometimes when we subject another person to Fixer behavior, they really *are* struggling, and we think we are helping rectify the problem. That's scenario one. In scenario two, we believe the other person is struggling, that they have a problem, when in fact they're perfectly fine. We think there's a problem when there is no problem, because *we* want the person to be doing something different, to be on a different path, even if they themselves do not feel stuck or unhappy.

Underlying Fixer behavior in both scenarios is the mentality that "I know better." Fixer Syndrome often masks itself as deep empathy and compassion, but it's neither of those—what it *is* is the insatiable thirst to know better than another person. In the case that a person we care about *is* struggling—they're unhappy in their job, they are in a difficult relationship, or a past traumatic experience continues to be impactful in a way that they acknowledge limits them from living as they wish, for example—and we insist that we know how to fix their problem better than they do, not only are we behaving as if we know more about the problem than the person living it, but we also lack acceptance. (And hint: believing that a person isn't doing what they should to address a problem automatically means you believe you know better, regardless of your insistence that you are "just trying to help.") The intention to fix always indicates our lack of acceptance. That lack of acceptance is a lack of acceptance both of the person and of the problem itself.

To truly connect to a person and to truly help them heal, you have to radically accept that person first. It's the same as it is with trauma: the number-one step toward healing trauma isn't to fix the problem; it's to accept the problem (remember, acceptance does not equal approval; it means ceasing to argue with reality). There has to be a radical, deep acceptance in your heart of both the person and the situation. It can't be an intellectual understanding where you know you should accept but still have lingering thoughts of fixing. There has to come a point where your view of the problem is no longer binary (the problem is bad and needs to be fixed, or the problem is now fixed, so everything's okay) but nondual: the problem is what it is, and your goal is to offer compassion through supporting them in the way they need, if they want that. Honestly, this can be as simple as asking, when a person comes to you with a problem, "Do you want solutions, or do you want comfort?" or "Do you want to vent, or do you want to problem solve?" Without judgment and fixing, you can try asking, "What are your needs?" You know you are in Fixer mode when you offer unsolicited advice to others. When people respond, "You don't understand" after sharing with you? Almost 100 percent, you were in Fixer mode. When people reject your help repeatedly? Guess what—you were almost certainly in Fixer mode again.

In the case of the second scenario, we're usually contending with two different ways of being in the world, two different perspectives, two different approaches to doing life. Maybe your partner works as a barista during the day in order to earn income, and in their non-income-earning hours, they write plays and are deeply involved in community theater. They are content, but you refuse to believe this. Your thoughts sound something like "How could they really be happy when money is tight/when they're not pursuing theater as a *career*/when they're so talented but not letting their light shine?" And as a result, you're constantly urging them to apply to grad school in theater or to network with a successful playwright you know through friends of friends or to apply for a job—any job—at a major theater in your city. These are all "fixes" for a nonexistent problem. These thoughts are about you and how *your* mind functions, about *your* needs in life. You are identifying a problem that doesn't exist and identifying what *you* perceive as a lack in your partner—ambition, though there is nothing inherently good or bad about ambition.

This desire to change someone is the opposite of accepting them. You're literally saying, "I want you to be other than what and who you are." This attempt to "fix" feeds into the idea that perfection exists—it doesn't. And it gives power to the judgmental side of you that thinks you know what's best for everyone. It is also a refusal to acknowledge that we each have different needs, different paths, stemming from our own unique, complex karmic momentum. Next time you find yourself thinking about how someone could improve their life, stop and focus on this desire as a mirror that reflects *your* values and needs. For example, if you want your loved one to change their job, ask yourself, "Would I be happy doing X job?" The answer is likely to be no, and this "no" is very useful—it signals that you are projecting. (If there is a slim possibility that the answer is yes, then it is possible that your loved one may be in need of change, but remember—your only job is to accept and support.) Doing this also helps to keep you in an expansive, rather than contracted, state by reminding you that your way of being is only one way to be in the interconnected multiplicity of being itself.

When it comes down to it, in either case, Fixer Syndrome is rooted in *superiority* ("I am better than you"), *judgment* ("You are not good enough"), *self-absorption* ("I know better") and *power* ("I can control"). As much as we think we're doing good, the impulse to fix is not rooted in love. One of the most complicated pieces of Fixer Syndrome is that you probably *are* a compassionate person, acting from the belief that you can prevent the other person from experiencing pain, suffering, or discomfort. However, none of us can control the reality that pain, suffering, and discomfort will come for us all at some point. And the Fixer Syndrome illusion that you're doing the right thing is so persuasive that it can be incredibly confusing and upsetting when the person on the receiving end of your "fixing" erupts with resentment and anger. You may think,

"What are you talking about? I've been helping you! I've been nothing but kind and generous to you," but you're so lost in the Fixer soup, you have no clue what you've done wrong. You've lost perspective and self-awareness. And, critically, what's missing from your approach is empathy and acceptance.

We must always actively remember that we don't know what it's like to be in someone else's head. We don't know what it's like to have the walls they have in their hearts. We don't know what it's like to live in their body. We don't know what it's like to experience the pain they are carrying. You must humble yourself to actively accept every nuanced layer of the person and of the problem, if there is one—both what you know of it and what you don't. You don't even have to say a word. At this level, it's your nervous system speaking to another person's nervous system: you are safe with me, you can be yourself, you are innately good, and I see your goodness.

Acceptance is an ongoing practice, not a one-time act that *poof* magically dissolves your desire to fix; it is a choice you make over and over again. It's a really hard practice, too, because it asks you to put the power back into another person's hands, even if *they* feel powerless. But once we accept without a shadow of judgment, then we can open ourselves up to the third truth, to making room for the *something else*, and find delight in it. Once we loosen our grip, *that's* often when we see change. It's no coincidence, I think, that people often see an ex finally make longed-for life changes *after* a breakup, like a better job, or a willingness to commit, or even just a haircut. And while it can be easy to resent that they didn't do those things when you were with them, the way of the universe is that freedom *from* often creates freedom *to*.

Fixer Syndrome is so seductive, though. I know this firsthand. I was a Fixer. Several years ago, my boyfriend at the time broke up with me, sick of my attempts to "help him," tired of my inability to *just listen* to what he was telling me. The breakup was devastating, and I was deeply heartbroken. Despite—or maybe because of—all the work I had done on my inner self and the self-awareness that came with it, the breakup took me by surprise (even though, deep down, I knew it was coming).

I didn't really understand the *why*; I didn't *get it*. When my boyfriend moved out of our house, I experienced a kind of loneliness I had never experienced in my life, not even as a closeted teenager in Brazil or in my twenties, when I slunk out of the NYC fashion industry in a cloak of shame.

One day after returning home from ecstatic dance class, I lay in bed and pleaded with my heart, "Please, tell me: what did I do wrong in this relationship? Why did he break up with me? What didn't work? Help me understand my faults; show me my part." My mind's eye began flashing images of all the times that I hadn't supported his needs, because I thought I knew better. The times I had not respected his boundaries in the way that he had wanted them to be respected, because I thought I knew better. The ways I had not honored him as a sovereign, strong, wise man, because I thought I knew better.

I did not know better.

With reflection, it became clear to me that I had been living in judgment of my boyfriend and making that judgment known through my "helpful" ideas about how he could be more "successful." Meanwhile, while he was looking for more direction on his path, he was looking inward, not toward me, for answers. I had thought, falsely, that because I was outwardly more accomplished by society's standards, that made me an expert on how to help my boyfriend. I had allowed *my* external reality to dictate how I engaged with someone else's internal reality. My thinking had been totally flawed. I had allowed my achievements and popularity to clutter my view of the fact that he had taken good care of himself throughout his life, that he had handled himself—without my meddling—just fine all along. It was really painful to reflect on how I had thought I knew what he really needed or should want—that because I'd had success in certain areas of my life, I knew how to help him get there, too, or even thought he wanted the same thing.

My boyfriend and I did eventually get back together (for a while), but I had to really commit myself to practicing acceptance, to remind myself that my work, my teaching and studies, didn't make me immune to Fixer Syndrome (and *might* just make me more susceptible to it).

I had to accept that we moved differently—my boyfriend liked to nap, and I never stopped moving. *And* he could read an entire book in a day, while it took me fifteen minutes to get through a single page (thanks, dyslexia). I'm an auditory learner, and he absorbed written information like a sponge. Unwavering acceptance of our many differences allowed me to see the third truth for us: the complementary nature of our differences, the give and take, the push and pull, the rhythm that kept everything moving between us.

Of course, you can accept that somebody is where they are and decide that's not where you want to be. Acceptance is never about complacency or becoming an enabler when it comes to damaging behaviors. You can accept somebody with love and with compassion and still determine that you don't want to be in relationship with them. When it comes to some people, you'll just have to say (using your inner voice here), "I accept you, and I genuinely love you, and right now the garden of my inner world isn't congruent with your gardening skills. So I have to remove myself and revisit someday when the time is right." (We do always have to revisit, though that need not be a literal revisiting of the relationship; it can mean simply making peace with the past in order to test the depth of our presence.)

It gets much trickier when you do want to remain in relationship with a person, but you feel that your needs are not being met. This is where things often get confused—when we conflate a desire to have our needs met with a desire to change another person. The two are not the same, though they might seem like it initially. Wanting someone to get a higher-paying job is not actually the same thing as needing help paying the bills (assuming here that you live with that person and you've previously agreed to share the financial burden of keeping the lights on).

The problem is, we have an inability to accept people while simultaneously knowing how to communicate that changes need to be made *to a relationship* rather than to a person. Focusing on your needs rather than on what's "wrong" with another person (i.e., what they need to change) is a relationship lifesaver that also builds our muscles of acceptance. Part of this means interrogating what's beneath your desire for the other person to change; remember that the desire is ultimately about what *you value*, and reframe it in light of that. Ask yourself, "Is 'I wish she weren't so messy' actually 'I need an uncluttered environment to avoid being overstimulated'?" What can your wish for another person to change tell you about your needs? What do *you* need, given who you are and how you're built?

The other part of accepting people while simultaneously communicating changes that need to be made to a relationship is expressing your needs with love and compassion so that it's truly about you and not a judgment of the other person. Because it's *not* about the other person. You can validate what is working if you wish, but your primary job is to communicate what you need simply and directly, from a place of neutral emotion (in other words, show up from a place of acceptance without judgment, blame, or resentment in tow): I need help getting groceries, I need my texts returned, I need plans to be made, I need more contact, I need help cleaning the house. Whatever it may be. When you do this, you're inviting the other person to meet you where you are. You're asking them to join you; you're holding out a hand rather than pulling it back—or using it to push them away. The key here is to have a boundary in place without holding on too tightly to an outcome. Say you have a close friend, but you don't feel totally secure in your friendship, you don't feel fully valued, because your friend frequently flakes at the last minute. You might tell your friend, "I need to spend more quality time together." And your friend responds, "I'd love that." Your next step is to be more specific about how you would like that need met while keeping the focus on you: "Okay, cool. Thank you for saying that, Drew—that means a lot to me. I do feel like, in general, I'm the one who usually initiates plans. And I feel disappointed when you cancel at the last minute. There have been three or four times this has happened recently, so can we commit to hanging out twice this month? And I'll initiate one hang and you'll initiate the next?"

What you're essentially doing here is setting up a time frame and a set of expectations—those are your boundaries, what you are or are not willing to accept. If you don't have healthy boundaries (boundaries that are neither too rigid nor too porous), you will have difficulty getting your needs met—you'll either be inflexible or let people walk all over you. So have a time frame, have an expectation for the need to be met in a way that you want, but never hold on to the outcome too tightly—it is a black-and-white truth that doing so will always make you miserable. When we talk about telling someone what we need and holding out that hand to them, we also need to be open to the possibility that the way they meet that need will not be the way we would have liked them to meet it.

Allow people to surprise you, and allow yourself to be open to having your needs met in ways that may not match your expectations exactly. There's a reason the Buddha emphasized the middle way in his teachings. Perhaps your partner isn't contributing financially in the way you need—but they do sit with you in creative meetings, and they've been essential in generating the theme for your next book. Maybe they're your first and best reader, full of insightful suggestions. They're awesome at iterating one idea after another. And this book is a hit. You're making money, drowning in praise, and receiving an outpouring of support from the universe. Yes, you pay more rent than your partner—but are you really going to break up with them because you think they haven't met your need (more evenly shouldering the bills)? They *have* met your need—their generosity with their creativity, their intelligence, and their time has been instrumental to your book's success.

In the end, so much of being in relationship is about getting our needs met, especially our core needs: the need to belong, the need to feel known and accepted, the need to matter, the need to feel safe. Needs are what guide and motivate everything we do in life. At birth and in childhood, we rely on others to meet most of our needs. But in adulthood, there are certain needs that you can only meet yourself: only you can meet the need to love yourself unconditionally, to take care of your body, to pick yourself back up when you fall. But doing so is expansive—in meeting your own needs, you practice meeting the needs of others and having yours met by them. When you meet your needs, you are being compassionate to yourself (preventing and relieving your own suffering).

As with anything, the more you practice it, the more habitual it becomes. Becoming compassionate to the self builds the habit of compassion in general. And when you're compassionate in relationship, you work to build a bridge that your friend or lover or family member can cross back to you.

Chapter 3

Be a Spiritual Gardener

When we talk about sacred friendship, about being a spiritual gardener, we're talking about two people working together to become free—in other words, to liberate and be liberated. Remember, no matter how much work you do between you and you, you can't get free alone. That's why the same old way we've been doing things—amassing as many "friends" as possible, seeking shallow validation, trying to fix people—has failed us so miserably when it comes to feeling truly connected. All of these habits and behaviors are rooted in conditioning that reinforces the delusion that we are separate—that not only our sorrows but also our joys are ours alone, and that relationship itself is ultimately a zero-sum game. When it comes to sacred friendship, though—when it comes to being a botanist of benevolence, of each other's basic goodness—getting it right means that you enter friendship rigorously oriented toward liberation so that within friendship, you can give your all, really dedicate yourself to being a radical lover, offering wise compassion, and delivering skillful honesty.

It's time. You've prepped your garden beds, you've filled them with nutrient-rich earth and tilled the soil—you've made yourself available for sacred friendship. Now you're ready to spot the invasive species taking over your garden—our culturally distorted ideas of friendship—and replace them with native plants, the fundamentals of sacred friendship. I've got *my* sun hat, my trowel and spade, and my gloves (they're flowered, if you're wondering)—grab *yours*.

Freedom and Friendship

Before we dive in here, my darling, there's something I really need to say first. And it's that, no matter where you are on this journey, you are worthy of love and connection. I say this because so many people I know believe that before they can be in relationship, they need to accomplish A, B, and C first (I mean all kinds of relationships here, but this is especially true of romantic relationships). The problem is, when you tell yourself this, you're signaling to your mind that you're not good enough, even if that messaging is wrapped up in the language of self-improvement and tied with a big red bow. You're sowing seeds of unworthiness in your karmic garden. I get it, though: the language of self-help is especially seductive when it comes to this seemingly obvious idea that being your "best self" is a requirement for attaining and being in relationship. I mean, it sounds kinda truthy, right? There's an intuitive gloss to the statement, a sheen of the self-evident. But it's not true, and it's also just wrong. First, it presupposes that you're not worthy as you are—wrong. Second, this "best self" is often couched in coded language that upholds a lot of gross stuff: ableism, classism, anti-fat bias. This "best self" is always a selling tool, literally—makeup, weight-loss programs, therapy apps, expensive nootropics for the hippie tech-heads—and figuratively, shilling superficial values that only feed the suffering cycle and that have nothing to do with being the "best" version of you.

Still, I *do* believe that being your "best self" is a condition of sacred friendship. It's just that we have some unlearning to do. We've got to interrogate just what the "best self" is. Because the inescapable truth is, no matter how much we exercise, how early we wake up, how productive we are, or how much we achieve, we still won't know our "best self" if *those* kinds of "improvements" (ugh) are our goalposts. It's only when we long for freedom—for liberation—and actively seek out its expression that we are our "best" selves. *The best self is the self in search of liberation.*

You have to be working on liberation to be a sacred friend. Do you remember that, at the very beginning of this book, I described liberation as freedom from our conditioning, freedom from the delusion that we are separate, and freedom to rest in the present with a fresh mind and open heart? Okay, well, it's really hard to practice the foundations of sacred friendship—being a radical lover, offering wise compassion, and delivering skillful honesty—when we're not free, i.e., when we're operating under the burdens of our conditioning (familial, cultural, religious, or otherwise), our obsession with individualism, and our incessant future-tripping and past-looping. Getting free is the work of a lifetime, a work that is multifaceted and always evolving (I mean, every page of this book is ultimately about doing that work), for sure. But when you read the word "liberation," I don't want you to think of it as some mystical, super-hard-to-achieve thing.

In many ways, liberation is as simple as stabilized present-moment awareness. Your mind is calm and concentrated. It's at rest. You are where your body is, and when you're there, you have access to your heart. So, in the context of "Spiritually, We," we could say the liberated self is a mind that is inhabiting the body. It's a heart that's wide open: someone who not only has the ability to take care of their own needs but is simultaneously bettering the world as they do so. Their consciousness has woven together being of benefit to themselves and being of benefit to others so that they are simultaneous undertakings.

When I'm not in a "Spiritually, We" state, I'm locked up in my preferences, my needs, my life. And that's what causes us to suffer—isolation, that view that we have to do life alone. When we are in the liberated mind, we understand that our pain is part of the collective pain, that our suffering is part of the collective suffering. And that our joy isn't our joy alone; it's part of the joy of the world, so it becomes our job to keep expanding and developing our joy, because it's not only benefiting us but also benefiting all people. The purpose of relationship is to help one another evolve, to be mirrors for each other, to see the goodness in each other, and to enjoy one another. Joy is an underrated quality in spirituality, but it is crucial. Enjoying yourself can plant the seeds for being enjoyed by others, experiencing joy in relationship. It's all connected, you see, and it starts with you.

Freedom is our true nature, but so much of what we have learned in life—the things we have been taught to value, like status, and the parts of ourselves we have learned to fear, like our vulnerability—goes against freedom. We don't know our basic goodness, let alone each other's; we don't know our authentic selves; we don't know our authentic joy. Instead, we live by our conditioning. Freedom is the limitless expression of who you are *underneath* all that. And it's when we long for freedom and actively seek out its expression that we are our best selves.

So much of our suffering, our lack of freedom, comes down to our conditioning. It's our conditioning that perpetuates the delusion that we're separate; it's our conditioning that makes us storify and pathologize, believe that we are our thoughts and feelings, fear living in the truth of ourselves. So breaking free of that conditioning is critical to being a sacred friend, to orienting ourselves toward liberation. Part of what makes breaking free so hard is that our conditioning is really, really good at alienating us from what we really value. When we don't know what we really value, it's easy to be blown here and there by the winds of our culture, to become untethered from the aspects of life that make it truly meaningful. So taking the time to stop and really focus, to get in touch with what we really value, is one of the most powerful ways we can escape the limiting perspective of our conditioning. And living in integrity with those values is one of our best tools for staying free.

Knowing what we value is also critical in *making* sacred friends—it's hard to surround ourselves with people who will act as botanists to our karmic gardens if our "picker is broken." If our values are superficial, we will attract the superficial. When I talk about values here, I'm not talking about some sanctimonious "family values" bullshit meant to shame anyone who doesn't conform to the hetero, middle-class, Christian American dream. I'm talking about your *deeply held beliefs about what really matters that, in theory, motivate your behaviors*. I say "in theory" because one of our greatest sources of suffering is that many of us don't act in alignment with our values, and that mismatch between what we say (to ourselves) and what we do causes us a lot of pain.

We might say we value "giving back" but spend all our free time watching Netflix while we scroll our phones internet shopping. There's nothing wrong with Netflix or buying cute shoes online, of course. But you're probably not going to be fulfilled or happy if you use most of your limited nonworking hours on either (or both). They'll leave you empty at some point. On the other hand, when our actions and behaviors match our values, we're living in integrity. I don't mean you need to volunteer with the elderly every Saturday (though that would be rad). But if you value community, for example, you should be looking for small ways, every day, to be a part of one. That could meaning learning your neighbors' names and walking a misdelivered piece of mail over to one of their houses. It could mean joining a running group. Whatever—the choice is yours. The point is that what you *do* reflects what you *value*. Or it should.

Of course, the problem is, a lot of us have lost touch with what it is that we truly value. When I left the fashion industry in 2012, I had been worshiping money-power-fame as my personal God for so long that I had no idea what I really cared about. My sense of self-worth came from my title, the money I could spend, and the contact I had with celebrities. If you had asked me, "What do you value?" or "What are your values?" I doubt I would have proudly replied, "Status!" But I don't know that I would have been able to reply at all. Back then, I never paused and asked myself, "What do I really care about?" I was so desensitized to the suffering in the world that I noticed the pain in it only if a fashion designer died. Seriously. My heart was not open to others. I was very fixated on a small fragment of society that I deemed "elite" and "worthy."

But my "success" was nothing more than a costume I wore over my wounded insides. I had completely lost touch with my authenticity. I didn't feel deserving of anything good. Everything felt like a performance. So I leaned in to the character of the eccentric, over-the-top, high-powered fashion mogul: surrounded by "friends," always up for a "good time," "the life of the party." My addiction was an insatiable monster. Nothing was ever enough for me. I always wanted more.

It wasn't until I was basically forced to leave, my tail between my legs, reeling with shame and fear, that I started to question how I was living. And then it wasn't until I went on a renunciate path, shedding everything I had thought defined me, that I really began to know myself. As I began letting go, I started to experience a deep heartbreak. I mourned how I had allowed the God of Greed into the most sacred place in my life. But the heartbreak helped me get curious. Questions came flooding in. What opens my eyes? What moves me? What gets my heart racing? What lights me up? What makes me cry? What am I inspired by?

I kicked the money-power-fame God off my altar and replaced it with the ultimate question: how free do I want to be? I let that question orient my mind day in and day out. I realized that I had unconsciously given mastery over my mind and my life to things that didn't actually matter. Suddenly I was awake and no longer desensitized. I explored what I cared about and started to live from those values, in integrity.

You don't need to go on a renunciate path to ask yourself these questions, to dig into the core of what you value—though heartbreak might lead you there, as it has a tendency to do. Heartbreak is often an invitation to surrender, to declutter, to renounce, to mourn that you have unfortunately and unconsciously regurgitated and replayed and recycled and copied and pasted other people's dreams as your own. But you don't need to be heartbroken, either. You can simply choose to do it. You can do it right now.

I'm not talking about writing down a list of your values here. You won't get anywhere that way. You'll be like, "Love." "Beauty." "Success." A bunch of abstractions. Those words sound pretty, but they're meaningless as lenses through which to assess how you're living your life—they won't help you understand what your values really are, let alone where they come from or whether you're acting in service to them. Love, beauty, and success are going to mean very different things to different people. They're not specific enough to be guideposts on your path of liberation. Instead, I want you to answer some questions. Open your notes app, grab a journal, flip a page on a yellow narrow-ruled legal pad with your favorite pen from Japan in hand (some of us need very specific tools when we do our creative work, what can I say?). However you do it, write.

These are the questions I want you to ask, though it doesn't matter what order you ask them in. Ask yourself, "Whom do I admire?" Come up with three names, say (again, there are no hard-and-fast rules here). They can be people you know in real life or not. The next thing

I want you to do is write down what you admire about each of them. Take as long as you want with each. Once you've got it all down, scan your answers and see if you can identify any commonalities between them. For example, maybe you wrote down Ruth Bader Ginsburg, your mother, and Ms. Jones, your childhood piano teacher. In thinking about elements they share in common, you note that they all forged an unconventional path in life for women of their generation. What did it take to do this? Bravery. Resilience. Commitment. Again, dig as deep as you need to. The idea is to unearth the values driving the behavior.

Ask yourself, "What do I want?" You can list as many things as you want, with the caveat that for each answer, you then need to ask, "What does that look like to me?" or "Why?" So, for example, if you write down "Success," you then need to describe what success looks like to you. Perhaps the answer is homeownership, a certain salary, and a family. In weighing this, consider what these can tell you about what really matters to you, like security (in this case).

Ask yourself, "When have I been most inspired?" By inspired, I mean those times you left a situation more energized spiritually, intellectually, emotionally, creatively, even physically, than you were when you went in. The world had an element of newness to it. You felt a sense of optimism, of hope, of possibility. As you identify those times, think about whom you were with, where you were, and what you were doing. Why were you inspired, and what were you inspired to do? Maybe it was as simple as, after coffee with a friend, the conversation made you see something in a new light, or you hadn't seen your friend in a long time and were reminded of their intelligence and self-awareness, or you were able to sit in truly companionable silence and appreciate the light filtering through the leaves in the back garden of a café. Perhaps you left and were excited to get back to a project you'd been stalled on. Try to identify the elements that contributed to the inspiration: connection, being at peace, exchanging ideas.

Ask yourself, "When have I been most fulfilled?" We're not talking about happiness here. Happiness is an emotion. If you're fulfilled, you probably do feel happy, but you can be happy without being fulfilled.

Fulfillment is an ongoing state of being in which you have a sense of purpose and you're meeting that purpose. Arriving there probably involved challenges and frustration as well as happiness. Again, think about where you were, what you were doing, and who was in your life.

There are a lot of other questions you can ask yourself to drill into your values—when were you most proud or what are your nonnegotiables, for example. As you examine the answers and look for patterns, you can start stacking them up against how you're actually living and spot the discrepancies or absences. You can ask yourself if your work supports your values. We all have needs to meet, of course—maybe your job is just that: a job that pays the bills. That's cool, too—are you supporting your values in other ways? But maybe your work is antithetical to your values and you realize you need to make a shift. Are your relationships a reflection of your values? Does your lifestyle reflect your values? As you gain clarity on your values, you can decide not only what matters to you but what matters most and what you can leave by the wayside. Maybe you'll realize that some of your values are inherited and no longer serve you (if they ever did). While our core values are likely to be lifelong companions, the priorities of those values are likely to change over the course of our lives as we grow and learn and unlearn and change ourselves.

Knowing what you truly value can help you understand who you truly are, which can help you resist the conditioning that perpetuates so much suffering. Your truest self comes from within, and knowledge of it comes from knowing your inner world—not from meeting the demands of conditioning. That is the true meaning of the "best self." Your best self is ever evolving because you are. The journey of self-discovery and self-inquiry is lifelong. But the arc of that journey is always bending toward freedom. So when you ask yourself if you're bringing your best self to a relationship or whether you have a best self to bring to a relationship (you do!), ask yourself these questions instead: how is the garden of my mind? What have I done today to plant healthy seeds and orient myself in the direction of liberation? What kind of karma am I cultivating? Am I high on my own bullshit? Am I ready to connect from my heart?

To be free requires ongoing work. You don't have an epiphany, become free, and boom—you're free forever. Our work becomes stabilizing ourselves in freedom: staying self-aware, testing our material, and checking in on the alignment of our values and actions. You don't suddenly become special (you already were special) when you choose and practice freedom. You don't get a license to brag about how free you are and how unfree others are. We all live in the world, and we're all subject to its conditioning. We don't need to judge ourselves or our friends for being human. Judgment and superiority have no place here—just orient yourself in the direction of joy, truth, and freedom whenever possible and do your best to surround yourself with other people walking the path.

Remember, we are the company we keep. From a Buddhist perspective, if you have virtuous friends, you will have a virtuous life. Don't be afraid to ask yourself, "Are my friendships liberatory?" A liberatory friendship doesn't expect you to be the same person today that you were yesterday; it frees you from the culturally hardwired tendency to believe in a fixed identity based on a linear, unchanging self. In a liberatory friendship, we accept that each of us is made up of infinite moving dynamic aspects coming together and falling apart, dying and being reborn. A liberatory relationship reminds you of your own constant destiny of full awakening. Liberatory relationships celebrate the impermanence of our difficulties and challenges, recognizing that we are all artists and that our own lives are our ongoing, collaborative works of art. In a liberatory friendship, you are challenged to grow; you are inspired; you are cared for, listened to, and held.

The more you start to orient yourself toward free people, the more you will become a freedom magnet but also a bullshit detector. In those relationships that are less free, you can offer the tools to become free by being deeply present with the other person. One of the main things we get wrong in relationships of all kinds is allowing ourselves to be ruled by our insatiable distraction. When we are distracted, we can't be in the moment. When we're not in the moment, we miss the poetry of life. And when we miss the poetry, we miss the opportunity to be the botanist, to bring goodness and beauty wherever we go.

When we're present, our minds are less sticky. We're able to let go more easily, we focus less on people's flaws. When we're present, we nonjudgmentally accept reality. Our vision is all-encompassing, nondualistic. This is freedom. The Sufi poet Rumi described this freedom when he wrote of a field "out beyond ideas of wrongdoing and rightdoing," instructing the reader to meet him there.[1] When we witness somebody, when we can be deeply present with another person, we are, like Rumi, inviting them to meet us in that field, to experience what it is to be free.

When you're free, you're not taken by your emotions, you don't believe every passing thought. You're able to be flexible in your mindset, to give and show love freely; you're not holding on too tightly, and you are curious about life with a beginner's mind. You're able to dance with impermanence and make peace with your past, no longer ruminating on it or regurgitating it into the present. You're no longer fearful about the future. You have the ability to be at ease with the fact that we're all going to die; you've made friends with your mortality. You have acceptance of the full human experience—the pain as well as the beauty. You seek facts but welcome mystery. You're living from your values, and our values are what make our hearts come alive.

Friendship Is for Lovers

Freedom from our conditioning makes it so much easier to give and receive both radical love and compassion, which together are the lifeblood of sacred friendship. When we're free from our conditioning, we're free from the delusion that we're separate, that we have to or even can do life alone. We understand our interdependence and interconnectedness, and it becomes more natural to love radically, to be compassionate.

From the perspective of traditional Buddhism, love and compassion are, in a sense, two faces of the same coin. At their essence, to love is *to work to support the happiness of another person* and to be compassionate is *to strive to alleviate the suffering of another person*. In both cases, what we're talking about here aren't feelings but *actions*. We take these actions because we get that the longing to be happy and the longing to be free of suffering are universal. For so many of us, though, wrapping our minds around the "actions-not-feelings" part can be challenging, *especially* when we're talking about love.

Okay, bestie, what *do* you talk about when you talk about love? Here in the West, we usually mean romantic love, which we exalt as a delirious emotion of unbridled joy, as a relationship in which we find another person who will meet all our needs, who will make us happy. We idealize them. And when they inevitably fail to meet those needs, when they prove less than ideal, we determine that the relationship has failed. Or when the passion has disappeared. Or when we no longer want to have sex with them. (All of which we almost always blame on the other person). Sound familiar? While we may have love for the person, we are no longer *in love* with them. Our primary goal is to *feel good*. It's all about me and my pleasure.

Honestly, our closest friendships, our relationships with our BFFs, aren't so different. We may not break up with them as quickly (although some of us ride an ever-changing carousel of friends, while we linger in romantic relationships too long), but much of our friendship is still founded on *their* ability to make *us* happy. Or we need ourselves to be their primary source of happiness—the ego must be satisfied. This kind of love, in which we externalize happiness as the responsibility of someone else rather than something we cultivate within, is pretty much the definition of attachment in Buddhism, and one of our primary sources of suffering. The Buddhist nun Jetsunma Tenzin Palmo describes it as "Attachment says, I love you, therefore, I want you to make me happy. Genuine love says, I love you, therefore I want you to be happy."[2] (Nuns always have the sickest burns.)

It's this kind of love-without-attachment that we mean when we talk about love as an act that supports another person's happiness. Love free of attachment doesn't require anything in return. It's unmotivated. There are no strings attached. It doesn't demand that people behave a certain way for us to love them. This kind of love separates the behavior of a person from their innate self. It's impersonal. *Wut.* What is this icy cold bullshit kind of love you're talking about? Impersonal love? Babe—that's what unconditional love is. It's not about the individual, i.e., what you like about them. It's not sentimental, and it can't afford to be, because it's rooted in the acceptance that we are *all* innately good. That's a tough space to hold in a culture riven by so many divides. Especially because when we accept our innate goodness, we must then accept, as I've said before, that humanity does not need to be perfect, to our liking, or without complication to be deserving of love. It is, and therefore, it is loved. You are, and therefore, you are loved. All living beings are enough, just as they are, and worthy of love. In Buddhism, the work of this love, or the love itself, is typically translated as "lovingkindness" (all one word; that's not a typo). But because the idea is so challenging to us, I prefer to call it "radical love." Accepting this idea of love requires us to *thoroughly* and *completely* overhaul our existing conception of love. In other words, it's a radical reimagining of what love can be and do.

Emphasis on *do*, honey. Radical love is a verb, it is a purposeful movement in our lives toward our shared humanity, it is the pull in each of us to take care of one another, to better this world. Radical love is not a feeling, it is an action; it is a choice to love in even the most difficult circumstances, in order to free the world—and ourselves. And in sacred friendship, babe, your job is to be a radical lover.

So do it. For most people, love goes where love already is. As a radical lover, you need to bring love where it is not. Be like the sun: the sun doesn't warm only certain people—where it shines, it shines on all. Where it shines, it illuminates all: the good, the bad, the ugly, the holy, the profane. This means you meet people where they are and support them as their complete selves. Love them through their shortcomings. Send love to their lateness. Send love to their texts left on read. Send love to their anger and their fear. In Buddhism, we believe every person has the potential to become a Buddha, and in doing so to become perfect—perfectly enlightened. But the fact is, not everyone is on that path, and if they are on it, I like to keep in mind that, as Mahatma Gandhi reputedly said, "The path is the goal." I also like to remind myself not to let the perfect be the enemy of the good, in the Western sense. Maybe you've hard this phrase, too. Usually, when we remind ourselves of this, it's because we're frozen by our own unhealthy Western-style, capitalistic perfectionism, which stifles our creativity, our energy, and our ability to act. But it's true of how we view others, too—when we hold others to some arbitrary standard of "perfect" behavior, we're rejecting their essential goodness. We're effectively saying they deserve love only if they meet X, Y, and Z conditions. No.

You are the sun. Shine that light on every little part of yourself. Bring warmth and illumination to every little part of yourself that isn't loved. Do this by accepting your inner goodness. Easier said than done, right? But it is very hard to truly accept others, to believe that others are innately good, if you're withholding this from yourself. After all, if *you* are not good, how can we *all* be good? You are inextricably part of the all. Accepting your goodness means looking at how you've lived and accepting it all, accepting your mistakes, your hurtful tendencies—owning that they happened and allowing yourself to recognize that that's reality. You can't change it. But you can remind yourself that the behavior is not who you are, and you can choose not to do that again. Acceptance is about dropping deeper past that top layer of our biography, past the external, and seeing that our harmful behavior, words, actions, mistakes were created from a misguided approach to fulfilling our needs to belong, to feel known and accepted, to matter, to feel safe. Anything that isn't in alignment with your highest good and the highest good of all people, bring acceptance to it as you acknowledge that you can't meet your needs for freedom, safety, and belonging in a skillful way unless you know that you are innately good, that your benevolence is always alive.

Hold on to that benevolence, because the moment that you start loving radically, everything that's beneath the surface that isn't loved will rise to the light, seeking to be loved—unconscious tendencies, automatic behaviors, thought patterns. Reframe challenging emotions as a call to live with radical love. Remember that the feelings that separate you, isolate you, shame you, scare you, and feed your neurosis, paranoia, and delusion are part of the collective suffering, and you are part of the collective. You're not alone in your suffering.

It's weird. When we're able to connect with the universal aspects of being human—like the fact that we all suffer and we all want to be free of suffering—we feel less alone. When we're in the depths of despair, though, it can be easy to believe "This only happens to me. No one else feels this way," when the truth is that what we're feeling is universal. When we believe we are alone in experiencing suffering, we end up shouldering the entire weight of its burden. But when we realize that our suffering has been and will be felt by everyone at some point, the weight of the load is lighter—it's shared. There's an element of relief. Yes, our experiences may be different, but we will all experience pain, because we cannot control life: death, illness, and heartbreak are part of living. And as a result of that pain, we all experience suffering. And yet we really, really shy away from the suffering of others.

Part of this is because of fear of contagion. We believe suffering is bad, and we don't want to catch it. The other part is denial: we don't want to believe suffering will come for us, so we tell ourselves that those who are suffering are somehow to blame. They must have done something wrong or bad, and we don't help bad people, right? Fear and denial are natural emotions, but they're anathema to radical love. That's why, as much as we're drawn to make a distinction between them, love and compassion are two faces of the same coin. Compassion helps us to love radically, and loving radically helps keep us in a state of compassion. The more we understand others, the more we understand our mutual goodness, the more we will want to relieve their suffering. And the more contact we have with suffering, with its universal nature, the more love we will feel for our common humanity.

You can't be a radical lover without practicing compassion. But like love, compassion isn't a feeling—it's not pity or sorrow or even empathy. It's *recognition* of suffering, followed by an *action* to relieve it. It's seeing things for what they are, and in this way, like radical love, it is impartial and impersonal. The desire to alleviate someone's suffering doesn't change even if they behave badly; acting compassionately isn't an action that requires anything in return, especially gratitude. Like love, compassion exists in the awareness of our imperfections and our innate goodness.

Compassion is living in the inquiry "What can I do to help alleviate our suffering?" Compassion aids us in understanding that the binary way we've been taught to see the world isn't the whole truth. Compassion affords us the capacity to disentangle behavior from the self, to recognize that someone's unwholesome or destructive actions are a consequence of their unique karma, a product of the inherited generational wounds that breed in all our family trees. Compassion reminds us of our shared pain, the nonnegotiable pain that comes with being human. It reminds us that with pain, there can be suffering, which can poison our perception and close our hearts to each other. It is our responsibility, as we awaken our radical friendliness, to cultivate compassion for every being. So much so that what we see as poison becomes medicine, the suffering of the world becomes inspiration, and the happiness in the world motivates us.

Critically, compassion allows us to love our imperfect selves fully. It reminds us that we, too, are products of our karma and transgenerational conditioning and are works in progress. Like Kintsugi, the Japanese art of mending broken pottery in which fragments of shattered vessels are pieced back together with visible seams of powdered gold, compassion transfigures our breaking points, rendering them beautiful elements of our wholeness. Compassion requires living in paradox—knowing that good people can make mistakes or actively do harm. Oscar Wilde wrote, "The only difference between the saint and the sinner is that every saint has a past, and every sinner has a future." I love this quotation because it speaks to the nonduality of being human, a nonduality that we can access through compassion: the idea that the only thing that separates the "blessed" and the "damned" is our perception—the saint was presumably once human and subject to human failings, i.e., a sinner; the sinner still has the freedom to become a so-called saint.

Practice: Tonglen Meditation

This meditation, which comes from Tantric Buddhism, works powerfully to awaken our compassion. The word "tonglen" means giving and taking. In this practice, you visualize taking in another person's pain and suffering with every inhale and sending them whatever will give them relief on the exhale. It's okay to feel nervous about this meditation or even turned off by it if you've never done it before—this is a pretty common response when I introduce it to my students. Many people feel that they just don't have the emotional energy to take on the suffering of another; their cup is empty. Or they worry that it's too big a risk to their own well-being, that a stranger's suffering will somehow contaminate their carefully guarded equilibrium. The surprise and the delight of the meditation, though, is the experience of transmutation it offers— how it refills your cup. Suffering becomes fuel. This is what it means for "poison to become medicine." As the late Tibetan Buddhist meditation master Chögyam Trungpa Rinpoche said, "The more negativity we take in with a sense of openness and compassion, the more goodness there is to breathe out. So there is nothing to lose."

Traditionally, you begin Tonglen by doing it for someone you care about whose suffering you wish to alleviate. But Tonglen can be done for yourself, it can be done for your "enemies," it can be done when your capacity for compassion feels limited. What follows is the classic four-step meditation, but the essence of Tonglen—breathing in someone's suffering and sending relief back out—can be done in the moment, on the spot, as you need it.

Sit comfortably and connect with your breath, resting your mind. Acknowledge distracting thoughts and emotions as they come up and let them go.

Now, connect your breath and your intention. As you inhale, visualize pain and suffering as a thick, dark smoke you're drawing into your heart to be transformed by the light of your compassion. As you exhale, visualize a bright, luminous beam of healing emanating out from you, transmitting relief and comfort.

Next, bring your focus to someone you know who is in pain or is suffering or to any painful situation that is real to you. Breathe in that pain, the sooty, dark, choking clouds of whatever it may be, and allow it to penetrate the walls around your heart, where it meets your compassion. Exhale the antidote to the pain, a silent blessing flowing as a river of light. For example, if you've called to mind a person who is struggling with disabling anxiety attacks, you can send them blessings of security and confidence.

Finally, extend your compassion outward. Extend it to all who are in the same situation. Breathe in the suffering of all who are grappling with that particular pain and transmute it on your exhale, sending them all the cool, fresh balm of relief.

Don't shy away from the suffering of others. Ask yourself every day, "What have I done to alleviate the suffering of others?" In friendship, this can be as straightforward as holding space for a friend in pain—making room for them to express their feelings, however uncomfortable they make you, while you listen without reacting. It could mean accompanying someone to a difficult event, like a memorial service or a doctor's appointment. It could be driving someone to the airport or picking them up after a hard trip. Here's the thing: there are usually pretty clear ways we can serve others when pain reduction is our goal, but it gets trickier when our goal is supporting someone to be happy.

Compassion and love can and do often happen simultaneously, of course. When someone is in distress, we often want to create a path forward toward a happier, more fulfilling life by alleviating their distress. But knowing how to support someone's happiness generally takes more skill, more wisdom, than alleviating their suffering. If someone falls off a ladder and can't walk, we drive them to the hospital, right? We don't second-guess them and start asking if they've considered that maybe it's actually their arm that's hurt or if they should go to a chiropractor instead. There's an instinctual element to our response to suffering; it's almost like we all suffer in the same ways. After someone has been in a car accident, we don't show up and ask if they've thought about changing careers. They're lying on the ground bleeding. We're not going to say, "Hey, have you thought about eating less sugar?" But when it comes to supporting someone's happiness, it's not about doing what *we* think will make them happy.

Friendship and Truth Telling

There's no magic trick to knowing what will make someone else happy. Fuck, we are often so far removed from knowing what will make *ourselves* happy. But one of the best ways to support someone else in their happiness is to *support them in their growth.* A big piece of that is knowing people will change and allowing them to change, not insisting that they remain tomorrow who they were yesterday. But the other huge piece of supporting someone's growth is having the capacity to communicate difficult truths. Just think how much growth would be possible if only we could really say to each other those things that are hard to hear. Hard to hear, but necessary.

Unfortunately, so many of our relationships are based on our conditioning and unprocessed emotional baggage. We have very little practice with skilled honesty, truth telling rooted in radical love and compassion, where the other person's welfare is top of mind. Instead, either we use "honesty" as a cudgel to hurt other people, or our fear of rejection leads us to avoid challenging topics. We hold back from addressing issues that need confronting, because we're frightened about how what we say will be received and what might happen in response: that we'll be alienated, cut off, left alone. Our unwillingness and inability to be a truth teller come back to that fundamental fear of being alone. We believe that being truthful would risk our friendships, and most of us are not willing to take that kind of risk. When you're focused on yourself and your own fear of rejection, you can't communicate honestly. And, duh—when your focus is yourself, you're not actually there for someone else.

I want my friends to straighten me out. Tell me if I'm off track. A fickle friend, a friend in the relationship for personal gain, a codependent friend, they're unable to do that. A sacred friend, a radical lover, though, speaks their truth even when, especially when, that truth is uncomfortable to share or hear, in service to their friend's growth. They speak with *skillful* honesty—that is, honesty that is motivated by the desire to support someone in becoming happy and to alleviate their suffering. Let me set things straight, though, honey: *honesty is no defense for being an asshole.* Seriously. Why do I even have to write that? Sadly, we *all* know those people who think it's *soooo* edgy to describe themselves as "brutally honest," who deliver rude and insensitive personal commentary that they follow with "What? I'm just being honest," or who accuse you of being "unable to handle the truth." These people are not beacons of honesty, they're being mean, and they hate being held accountable for the impact of their words. They're also not delivering any "truths," it should go without saying. We can always speak only to *our* experience of a person's behavior. Our thoughts are built on our lived experience, right? My perception of you is built on what I've lived through life. It has truth, but it's not *the* truth.

So how do you know if you're not an asshole? Being skillfully honest with others begins with being fiercely honest with yourself. Before you broach a hard topic with your friend, ask yourself if you're about to say what you're going to say because they're not obeying the script you wrote for them in your mind. So much of our suffering in relationship comes because of this unconscious scripting. We fear that if people go off script, we'll be hurt. If we can control how people respond to us, however, we'll be safe. The need to control is a common response to trauma. We lost control, or we never had control, in the traumatizing event or events. So now it's "let me find control."

We all struggle with this Main Character Energy problem. We assign people roles in the movie of Me. We tend to have a myopic view of life in which we exist at the center of reality, and we imagine that everybody else is an actor in our movie. But there is no movie in which you, or anybody else, is the star. There's just one overlapping movie in which your job is to be an improv actor. In this improvisation, you're eliminating suffering and inviting happiness. You're inviting the other actors who are doing this movie that we call life into their truth. The conversation isn't about shoulds and absolutes; it's about pointing in the right direction and inviting exploration—like the famous Zen Buddhist saying, it's not about the moon, it's about the finger pointing at the moon. If you're looking for an outcome, you're seeking to control. You're still holding on to your script, driven by your attachments.

Speaking and hearing the truth is a dance. To call yourself a radical lover, you have to be someone who can receive feedback without becoming discombobulated, regardless of the nature of it. I think we all know that hearing something we perceive as negative about ourselves can send us into a spiral. But if we pay attention to our bodies, our systems also light up when we hear positive messaging from another person. Being able to listen without reacting means you're not agitated either way. You have the capacity to hear and be present in a calm and relaxed body. That requires real work.

Part of the work is being in your body and staying connected to your breath. We can never hear somebody else's perspective about us if we're not relaxed—it just won't land. If we're not in our bodies, if we're not connected to our breath and our present-moment awareness, there's no way we can receive their truth without the distortion of duality. When we're occupying the realm of nonduality, that's the space—the only space, really—in which feedback isn't good or bad—it just is. It's just information to be observed and processed in service to our growth. That's the freedom piece, right?

And the other part of the work is holding on to your inner goodness. It's not that you're not elated about or appreciative of positive feedback or dismayed about negative feedback, but because you know that you are innately good, you don't take it *personally*. It's not personal in the sense that it doesn't touch your goodness. It's not personal in the sense that it doesn't touch your spirit. Reality is present-moment awareness—that's all you are. Spirit is your present-moment awareness. What happens, though, is that we get confused about this awareness— reality is present-moment awareness, yes, but it's the consequences of your actions (and your past-life karma/generational trauma) that lead to the karmic momentum of your present reality that's being observed. We get lost and confused in the observation, because we're habituated to identifying with, personifying, and storifying what we're seeing. The work of the liberation path is to disentangle ourselves from the idea that we are our actions, that we are our thoughts, that we are our emotions, that we are our stuff. To stay present, then, you need to hold on to two things, to remind yourself *I am innately good*, and *I am present-moment awareness, shining a light on what is coming up as a consequence of the past.*

While we can't inhabit somebody else's body or mind, we can tune in to their energy. We *know* when someone is not in a place to hear something hard; we can sense it in their body language, in the quality of their focus and attention. It goes without saying that if the other person isn't in a relaxed state—if they're already defensive and distracted—if they're in a bad place energetically, then this isn't the time to deliver hard truths. Whenever we're in conversation, we're always bringing our baggage to it. The only way for that baggage not to drag us down and away from hearing is to be in that relaxed state. As the "truth teller," you need to check in with yourself before you speak—are *you* in an embodied and relaxed state? Can you release all of your conditioning, all of your desire to control the outcome, and instead just be a mirror in which your friend can see themselves with new clarity? Don't be afraid of what they're going to see, or you won't be able to invite *them* to look at their reflection without fear. This is when the love piece comes in; this is when the compassion piece comes in. This is when you have to be honest with yourself that you might not be coming from the right place. Maybe you're agitated. Maybe you haven't been compassionate with yourself. Maybe you haven't been loving yourself skillfully. Once you have been honest, compassionate, and loving toward yourself, then you can create that connection where you're dancing together in a nonverbal way. Then the mirror is a natural thing; the conversation is the mirror that reflects a pattern.

The wish to support someone in being happy—to love them deeply, that is, radically and unconditionally, free of attachment—is to support them in their growth, in whatever it is that helps them, ultimately, experience liberation. But that is not a growth that we can ever force or foist upon them. Our part is limited to being a catalyst of change. Remember, we're all improv actors in the joint production that is life. We can't write the script for others, but we can collaborate. In real-life improv theater, there is a game actors play called "Yes, And." Just the name is beautiful, right? It's both affirmation and possibility, simultaneously. In the game, one actor begins by inventing a scenario, and their partner must agree to that scenario, to that reality—that's the "yes"—and then riff on it—that's the "and." It's a process of collaboration and trust and invention, one that rebuffs predictability and requires a certain amount of faith. When you decide to be a sacred friend, to become a radical lover, you're saying "yes, and."

We can't write the script for others, but we can collaborate. Radical love is an act of collaboration, a profoundly creative joint labor. Yeah, *labor.* Look, it's literally right there, snuggled at its center: col**labor**ate. The idea of work, of effort, of action, is built into the language itself: *col*, a Latin suffix for "with" or "together," and *laborare*, "to labor." If radical love is an act of collaboration, of working together, we understand that love itself is a form of labor. As civil rights leader, activist, and author Valarie Kaur wrote, "Love is a form of sweet labor: fierce, bloody, imperfect, and life-giving—a choice we make over and over again."[3]

Becoming a radical lover is a destiny available to all of us—believe it or not, we're all oriented toward liberation. Some people might get there faster, sure, while for others, it might take years, a lifetime, or many lifetimes. Along the way, as we walk the path of liberation, as we grow and evolve, we can *choose* our relationships, ones grounded in love and compassion. And we must choose how to *be* in those relationships. None of us are going to be perfect at friendship at all times. Friendship, the basis of any close relationship, is hard work that requires radical love, compassion, and honesty—real person-centered, not self-centered, love. Yes, you need to work on yourself in order to be available for sacred friendship, but you must simultaneously engage with others in the world—in connection with others is how you realize your insights. Even when we practice solitary work, we need to remember that it's with the purpose of going back into society and sharing what we have uncovered. Sometimes the keys that come to us in solitary may not only free us from our own prisons but also prove to be the breakthrough one of our friends needs. At the end of the day, we are in service to one another.

A sacred friendship is a spiritual contract—as are all relationships. It is in relationship that we test our skills—yes, maybe you've done the work between you and yourself to reach a place of body neutrality, to stop the negative self-talk about what you see in the mirror, but are you still engaging (even if only internally) in body shaming others? Are you still judging a person's worth, their morals, their will based on their appearance? You can only know if you've truly grown, if you've truly changed, in the context of relationship. It is in relationship that we learn new ones, that we learn the ultimate qualities of acceptance, love, and compassion. It doesn't get any more spiritual than that. We tend to each other's spiritual gardens; we are each other's karma. Sometimes we are student, sometimes we are teacher, but we are always equal. We hold up mirrors for each other to illuminate the darkness and increase our orientation toward the light. It is through friendship that we heal the deepest places within us.

Chapter 4

Conflict Is for Lovers

Even when we understand what sacred friendship is meant to be, how it should function, why do we still so often struggle to connect? Because, sweetheart, we expect it to be easy—we imagine it shouldn't require, you know, *effort*. It shouldn't be *laborious*. Good things aren't work, right? Yeah, yeah, yeah, I've heard the same cliché as you a million times: relationships take work. Doesn't the fact that so many people believe this prove I'm wrong? Sis, the almost religious way people recite that as if it were an inalienable truth only proves my point: our attitude toward relationships is actually pretty negative. "Relationships take work" is mostly used to justify weaponizing our emotions as normal, to normalize the dysfunctional relationships so many of us are in and perpetuate.

We *expect* long-term relationships to be frequently hard and unpleasant (and honey, a lot of them are, but more on that in a minute), and describing them as "work" reflects that. Here in America, where most of us have to work, work, work just to make it day to day, where we learn that our self-worth correlates with our productivity, where many of our most socially necessary and valuable jobs (teaching, caretaking, etc.) are treated as disposable, where wealth is hoarded and rest is hard to come by, work is something to dread, not celebrate. "Work" is loaded with negative connotations, bristles with tedium, exhaustion, obligation. It's not a matter of choice. And our relationships, including our friendships, are "work," mostly because our poor relationship to conflict gets in the way of real connection.

Yes, our relationships *are* frequently hard and unpleasant—dysfunctional—because most of us don't know how to handle conflict in a healthy way. Good relationships do take work. Sacred friendship does take work. It is sweet labor. That *doesn't* mean relationships should be full of strife. It does mean accepting that even when you love someone, even when you get along really well, even when you share similar values, life is going to serve up things that are uncomfortable, hard, painful, unpleasant. Those could be misunderstandings between people, mistakes we make, events in our lives that are hard to deal with. In other words, life is going to serve up conflict. Doing the work of sacred friendship means that you do what needs doing to sustain the relationship, that you do the work of a sacred friend—loving radically, with compassion and skillful honesty—even when life serves up difficult conversations, when life serves up loss.

Instead, for so many of us, because conflict is so deeply uncomfortable, we respond to it from a place of panic, thoughtlessly and without self-awareness. When the clash happens, it's not two (or even one) self-aware people, two radical lovers, seeking perspective; it's two people speaking shadow to shadow, subconscious to subconscious, automatic behavior grappling with automatic behavior. Most of us fumble through conflict, triggered, our emotions running high, our cortisol pumping; our old, played-out stories leading the charge; *or* we run away—avoid, avoid, avoid!—sheltering behind rigid boundaries. Sometimes the boundaries are the response to the trigger, a response to a pattern that becomes a pattern itself. Behind it all, the fear. Fear of discomfort, fear of rejection, fear of loss.

This might land harsh af, but I have to tell you: the point of life isn't really to be happy. That's different from being free. In my community, I see people all the time who preach spiritual enlightenment but who live lives verging on the hedonistic—for them, despite what they espouse verbally, the pursuit of pleasure is the ultimate goal. There's nothing wrong with living a happy life, but if that means avoiding all people and things that make you uncomfortable, you've totally missed the point of life on earth. Worse, it means you operate without the possibility of compassion, which requires the recognition of suffering—not just in others *but in all of us.*

Avoidance of conflict might feel like a survival tactic, one you adopted in good faith, but all it does is prevent connection while cultivating blame and allowing you to deny responsibility for your own actions and unloved trauma. The avoidant behavior that runs rampant in our society simply reinforces the idea that escaping the present moment is somehow advantageous. And as you know, you can't get free—there's no liberation to be had—if you can't be present. Avoiding conflict is personal development, not spirituality. You know, because it's all about *me.* My life. My feelings. I matter more than you do. Being in conflict is part of the spiritual path. Avoiding pain, avoiding loss means avoiding life itself.

To be a sacred friend, to be in any relationship, we can't run away from pain, from loss, from discomfort. We can't avoid it. We have to be willing to engage. We have to run toward life. We have to show up for what's difficult, as much as we have to show up for what gives us pleasure. My love, conflict is a part of every relationship—every romance, every friendship, every family dynamic. Because, in life, we're going to disagree. We're going to misunderstand each other. We're all showing up on this plane with our unique karma. We're going to have needs, values, goals, motivations, perspectives, and preferences that are not always perfectly aligned with those we love (or simply tolerate).

There's been so much written about healthy versus unhealthy conflict, but what if we acknowledge that conflict itself is just neutral, without inherent value? It's what *rises between two people* when we can't quite keep it copacetic. Let's save the healthy and unhealthy labeling for how we respond to conflict. I bring this up because maybe, just maybe, if we could bring some third truth energy to conflict—there's good, bad, and *what is*—we wouldn't be so fucking afraid of it. Maybe if we could bring some third truth energy to conflict—recognizing the spiritual potential of what we don't know and making room for the *something else*—we would see the creative potential of conflict, the possibility it offers us to build connection, to deepen understanding, with each other but also with ourselves.

If It's Hysterical, It's Historical

In recovery, people come to learn that as addicts, our outsized responses to experiences that don't seem to warrant full-blown meltdowns (which we then usually self-medicate into submission) are really about *the past,* not whatever is happening in front of us. "If it's hysterical, it's historical" is practically a mantra in AA. And look, while I'm not supercrazy about the word "hysteria" given its history as a tool to gaslight women, I embrace it in this phrase because of the loss of control it suggests, the disproportionate reaction, the gender-neutral explosion of emotional panic, and its clear relationship to the histories we carry within us.

You don't have to have had a routine Wednesday-night blackout at your local Lower East Side Bar, a very expensive designer drug habit, or a good old-fashioned pill addiction to embrace the idea that oftentimes, the way we feel about and relate to certain present-moment experiences has little to nothing to do with what's actually happening. The problem is, this would mean coming face to face with our trauma or having to accept a degree of responsibility for our emotions. It's so much easier to point the finger at someone else, to lay blame at the feet of the person who "made" you mad, angry, rageful, "hysterical," especially in conflict. Welcome to the realm of triggers or, as I like to call it, weaponized deflection.

To be clear, I'm not talking here about true mental health triggers, those often unpredictable sensory stimuli that resurface traumatic experiences as if they were actually happening, causing a person to become emotionally or physically reactive. And I'm not talking about the types of triggers that can activate or worsen the symptoms of disorders like OCD. What I *am* talking about is our culture's increasingly casual use of the word "trigger" to describe anything or *anyone* that causes a person discomfort or other strong emotions. We often justify avoiding conflict—avoiding relationships in which we believe conflict will arise—by labeling people as triggering.

Be honest, have you ever said of someone, "X triggers me"? And I get it—whoever they are, it probably feels like you can't help but react to them in a certain way. Seeing them, talking to them, being around them arouses difficult emotions (depending on who they are and your history with them, the strength and texture of those emotions will vary, of course). So you avoid them. You avoid conflict. In a sense, sure, they're triggering you. Literally, a trigger is a mechanism, like a switch, that initiates the operation of a device (like a gun or a power tool). And it's interesting, because you need to apply only a small amount of pressure to a trigger to release a much greater force of energy, you know? So, yes, it can feel like a person is flipping a switch in you—pushing your buttons. It can feel like the littlest thing they do sets you off. Notice, though, how the phrase shifts the action to the other person—*they* trigger *you*—implying your passivity and lack of agency. But here's the thing: the trigger, the switch, the button *is in you*.

The trigger already lives in us—if it's hysterical, it's historical.

Anytime someone triggers you, your reaction is rooted in seeds that were already sown in your karmic garden. It is rarely, if ever, about the other person; it's about how we relate to life, and in this sense, triggers are a conditioned response. Triggers, then, are a signal that we have some weeding to do, that our gardens could use a little care and love. They point us in the direction that needs tending, alerting us to where our work lies. Triggers reveal the parts of ourselves that are unsettled and unhealed. If we're willing to look at the anger, the sadness, straight on, we are gifted with the opportunity to love ourselves better. In a sense, people who trigger us are our best teachers—if we allow it, these moments can be the lessons that, once learned, help evolve our karma.

When you're hysterical, though, you *label* the people in front of you. They're toxic, they're poisonous, they're the culprit behind all your pain and suffering. They are the sole reason your life is miserable and you feel miserable. When you do that, you miss the fact that the rage and discomfort rising inside you were inside you to begin with. That person, the feeling of conflict, that experience, that event, those circumstances that came together were the last little bits of water and sunlight the seed inside you needed to break through the soil and sprout. If that seed of despair or jealousy or anger hadn't been there all along, you might relate differently to that person, regardless of what they said or did.

You *could* receive triggers with compassion for yourself, with the understanding that something exists in you that is asking for your attention. Instead, we too often respond by ignoring that part of ourselves and avoiding situations in which we can't help but be aware of it. Triggers we don't attend to can easily take over our karmic gardens, dictating our actions and responses to large swathes of our lives. What we avoid, we give free rein to.

A friend of mine recently confessed to me that she had almost blown up at a young woman with a baby while waiting in line at the cash register of a local grocery store. The line was long and moving slowly, and my friend had been in it for about fifteen minutes already. It was the end of a long day, and she still had to get home and make dinner before staying up to finish a project for work. There was just one person ahead of her when this young woman appeared and seemingly cut the line, muttering, "Excuse me, sorry," without waiting for any kind of response. My friend didn't have the chance to say, "Hey, I've been waiting here for fifteen minutes, and so have all these other people."

In an instant, she was filled with rage. Fully formed narratives suddenly sprang up in her mind: the young woman was a drug addict, a single mom, and an all-around bad person. The ugliest train of thoughts entered her mind, thoughts that reflected the worst of her biases. Her vision narrowed and her heart rate skyrocketed. On the verge of what felt like a blackout, my friend realized that she had completely ghosted the present moment and started to come back into her body.

As she did so, she became aware that the young woman was hugging the woman who was in line in front of my friend. It was her mom. The baby in her arms was the woman's grandson. And the mom hadn't seen her daughter and grandson in a little while because of COVID. My friend felt sick with embarrassment and hung over from the adrenaline that had shocked her system. After paying for her groceries, she sat in her car for a bit, in disbelief that she had just projected so much hate into the world—and at the thoughts that had surfaced within her.

She told me that later, her therapist responded to the situation by saying, "Oh, you were triggered because you grew up with a single mom," and then down into history they went. For my friend, this felt like a truth that landed. It gave her something to hold on to, and she felt less guilt and shame about her thoughts surrounding the young woman. While this felt like a breakthrough in the moment, it was simply another person to blame for her feelings, removing responsibility from her. This line of thinking kept her in a state in which she lacked any autonomy, in which her mom was at fault for my friend's behavior.

Excuse me? Bitch, didn't you just tell us, "If it's hysterical, it's historical"? If that's your inner dialogue right now, I can't say I blame you. But, honey, when I'm talking about how we need to be aware that we're constantly regurgitating the past into the present, I'm not talking about losing yourself in the psychoanalytic rabbit hole. Talk therapy can be an amazing tool for healing—it's often the first context in which we recognize patterns in our life and thus have the chance to break them. And speaking to a skilled therapist, who holds space for the full array of our imperfect human experience and listens without judgment, can radically minimize the shame we feel. But talk therapy is also very much about stories and narratives, which usually require a villain, keeping us in a blame mindset. Releasing that mindset does not mean absolving someone of their responsibility for the harm they may have caused. It does mean owning that you and you alone are responsible for your actions in the present. Stories and narratives are also about how we *feel* about what has happened to us, our *thoughts* about the people and events. In this way, they can reinforce the delusion that we are our thoughts and feelings.

They also don't leave much room for the third truth—the way I see, the way you see, and *what is*. For my friend, her mom made bad choices (getting pregnant and dropping out of college) and didn't measure up to the other mothers she saw in her friends' lives. But her mom probably had an equally persuasive story: she worked two jobs not only to make rent and put food on the table but to be able to rent in a good school district, to give her daughter piano lessons and send her to cheer camp, to make sure she had new clothes every year.

If you're feeling resistance as you read this, that's okay. That's natural. I know some of you are probably thinking, "But my mom really was horrible!" Yes, some parents never healed enough before having children. Those parents can and do cause terrible pain in their children's lives. Nothing we're talking about here invalidates that truth. Maybe not having them—or other triggering people—in your life is the right path for you. Sometimes it's necessary to cut people from our lives, to step away from them with the acknowledgment we can control only the work we do on ourselves. They might be our teacher, we might be the student—but hey, remote learning is a thing now.

The problem is when we lay responsibility at the feet of another for our actions *now* and when we label these people as bad or toxic. In rejecting their essential goodness, we cultivate karma that is as far from beneficial as it can get. And if you're in the habit of labeling people this way, I can also *guarantee* that you speak to yourself in the same reductive way—lacking compassion and imprisoning yourself in essentialism. What are you calling yourself when you're alone? Next time you're triggered by a person, see if you can remind yourself, before the hysteria sets in, that *just like me, they want to be happy. Just like me, they want to be free of suffering.*

We've become profoundly fragile, but our hypersensitivity has not become the bridge to an openness of heart. In fact, this hypersensitivity oftentimes prevents connection. Fragility is yet another way to bang the door of your heart shut, a way to make assumptions about others really quickly and let your biases act as your full perception. Too often in our relationships, we identify people as triggering or cut them off for offenses that could or should be met with grace—our response is not in proportion to the event (hysteria). A friend posts something cringe on social media, they say something with which you disagree, they do something annoying—they're triggering. They're toxic. You're done with them. Doing so feels like the right move in a culture celebrating cancellation (rather than accountability, which might require communication, which might involve conflict), but it's the polar opposite. Our rigidity and inflexibility when it comes to others are keeping us from connection. They're keeping us isolated. They're keeping us stuck.

Quieting the Hysteria

So can we learn to interact with a triggering person without being activated? Yes. Pain will happen inevitably, but with suffering—how we respond to the pain—we have a choice. Ultimately, you need to ask yourself, "How free do I want to be? Am I committed to being free or to being right? Am I committed to peace or to anger? Do I actually want to be a sacred friend and have sacred friends?" Seriously, have that tough conversation with yourself, interrogating your answers with skillful honesty. Are you willing to stick through the hard parts: actually acting in service to those goals when it's not easy to do so, choosing to do the work even when—especially when you're triggered—intense emotions catch fire? For now, because you're reading this book, I'm going to operate on the assumption that you *do* want to be free, you are committed to peace, and *yes, yes, yes*, you do want sacred friendship. And you're here for the heavy lifting.

Good thing you've been practicing. Because you have. So much of our ability to attend to our triggers and receive their lessons, rather than becoming hysterical and blame oriented, is about relying on our skills as radical lovers and our training in paradox and utilizing them in conjunction to stabilize ourselves in a higher perspective of the mind—to be rock steady at that thirty-thousand-foot view. This stabilized perspective allows us to receive the lessons, the messages, that difficult people deliver and prevents us from descending into the soup of condemnation and recrimination.

Remember when I said that our reactions to triggers are rarely, if ever, about the other person; they're about how we relate to life? Let's focus on that "relating to life" bit—because this is where the difference between therapy narratives and what we're doing here comes into play. Well, what are we doing if we're not looking at our past and trying to pin the source of our actions on our personal histories? First, we are agreeing that while our pasts may *inform* our behaviors, our pasts do not *cause* our behaviors. Second, we are reminding ourselves that triggers are a type of conditioned response: the stimulus is arbitrary (it's not about them) and our conditioning is at play—it's our job to get free. Finally, we are bringing focus to the understanding that how we relate to life is not just about "what happened to me" but about our *karma*.

Each of us shows up planetside with our accumulated karma, and each of us lives in a moment of karmic possibility, right? How we relate to life (in other words, how we relate to our experience of the present reality and what we choose to do with this moment of karmic possibility) is created by the consequences of our previous actions *and* the actions of those versions of ourselves from previous lives. When we hold close the knowledge that how we relate to life is about our karma, we are not only focusing on the consequences of our actions (as opposed to the actions of others), but also, and more crucially, we're in touch with a higher per-spective of mind, one that sees itself spanning many lifetimes. From this vantage point, we are aware of the self-as-process, rather than as a fixed identity, and that this process you call "me" or "I" didn't start with you. Our karmic momentum, i.e. how we react to life, in part predates us. But it's up to us to steer our karma in the right direction going forward.

This higher perspective of the mind is inherently radical, almost miraculous, in that it's a complete change from our everyday perspective on the "self," which is very time bound and invested in the ego. The higher perspective of the mind opens us up to see what we weren't able to see before: the unattached nature of the ongoing process we call self and the goodness at its core. This understanding builds our capacity to differentiate behavior from the self. We can recognize that when people act in unwholesome, unskillful, and destructive ways, they are living out their karma. The lessons are theirs to learn, or not, in this lifetime or the next. It's not our place to assign ourselves the role of teacher.

Recognizing our inner goodness and differentiating behavior from the self is radical love in action, of course. To be able to love someone radically is to be able to say of them, "Yes, that person did something fucked up, *and* they're not bad." We are at peace living in paradox.

And when we live in paradox, we understand that the way we see the world isn't the whole truth. There is always room for the possibility of something else.

When someone triggers you, you have to draw on your practices of radical love and embracing paradox and rest in that higher-mind perspective. This is for you and them. We extend radical love, comfortable in a state of paradox, to those we find challenging, because we can't afford not to. That's the "for them" part. Here's what I mean: when you encounter a person who causes harm or hurt or discord, you have to understand that *they* are hurt. This is not about sympathy or forgiveness or a personal response. It's about understanding that if they were at peace with themselves, they would never harm another human being. Knowing they're hurt does not excuse the behavior, but it does make it clear that if we want them to stop hurting others, it's imperative that we act to support their healing (and healing requires accountability). Hurt people hurt people.

For *you*, loving radically, embracing paradox, and resting in that higher-mind perspective quiets the hysteria that a trigger activates. In that quiet, you can better release a blame mindset, you can turn your focus from the outward to the inward, and you can then better accept ownership of the trigger itself. When our triggers are "pulled," parts of our psyche that we haven't been willing to see activate and surface. We then have this amazing opportunity to actually disrupt a pattern, to seize the opportunity for transformational growth, for becoming a better friend, partner, and family member.

Does this all sound a little too abstract, a little too "good in theory"? Let's make it concrete. Literally, the next time you find yourself triggered by someone or you know you're going to encounter someone you consider triggering, take a breath. Center yourself in your body. Silently recite the truth of our common humanity: *just like me, they want to be happy; just like me, they don't want to suffer*. Attend to the trigger. What are the thoughts flashing through your mind about this person? Now, drop the stories and focus on what you are actually feeling. Observe the feelings, separating them from the stories and from the other person.

Observe the feelings until you notice a natural change happen: they pass. A wider perspective dawns in you. The more you practice being with your feelings, free of the stories, the more powerless the stories become, because you have removed their emotional charge. Slowly, the old emotional baggage that haunts your present moment fades away. You are no longer the angry mess you used to be. Those feelings live in you, but they are not you. Carl Jung, the Swiss psychologist who developed the theory of archetypes (the universal symbols or patterns present in the collective unconscious of all humans) wrote, "Everything that irritates us about others can lead us to an understanding of ourselves."[1] Open yourself to seeing triggers as a reflection of something inside that needs your attention.

Accept that triggers are often a form of conditioning that needs to be questioned. Don't let your unprocessed emotional baggage dictate how you feel about an experience in the present moment. Don't let adopted fragility—the sense that you should be outraged and harmed by the most minor of infractions—become an unwanted shield blocking your heart. Next time you consider cutting a person out of your life, ask yourself if by doing so, you're actually establishing a necessary boundary or if you're maybe, *just maybe*, engaging in spiritual bypassing—avoiding the discomfort of following your triggers to where they lead, avoiding the discomfort of making room for the thorny but human flaws and foibles of others (and thus your own), avoiding the discomfort of living with the third truth and thus ultimately missing its possibilities, benevolence, and grace.

Peace Cannot Be Kept by Force

My close friend Johnny and I shared a mutual friend, Sam. For me, Sam was a fun person to have brunch with but not part of my inner circle. Sam was Johnny's best friend, though—right up there in the core five, ride-or-die, in-it-till-the-end type of friend. They'd met the first day of college and had been almost inseparable for the better part of two decades. Sam was well known for his explosive temper but had been working on it since getting sober five years earlier. To most people in our friend group, he appeared to have transformed his life and how he treated people, and it's fair to say that for the most part, he had. When it came to Johnny, though, Sam still had episodes of being emotionally abusive—almost like Johnny was his safe place to act out, knowing that Johnny would never "break up" with him. And for Johnny, this made him feel special; it confirmed that no one else was as close to him as Sam and that they shared a bond with each other unlike either one had with anyone else. Codependent much? *Anyway*. We don't need to get into the psychology of their relationship, which had outlasted multiple boyfriends and even a marriage, except to say there was a lot of love there.

So it sent a shockwave through our friend group when Johnny, seemingly out of the blue, stopped speaking to Sam. From the outside looking in, it was inexplicable that their friendship of fifteen-plus years had evaporated overnight. However, I knew that for every six or seven times Johnny and Sam spent together, there'd inevitably come an incident in which Sam belittled Johnny, or gaslit him, or cold-shouldered him, or unleashed on him, or delivered cutting insults with little to no emotion. For Johnny, these episodes triggered feelings of worthlessness, amplified his need to people please, and inflamed his anxiety. This was made worse by the fact that he never knew which Sam he would get. For the entire duration of their friendship, Johnny realized, he had felt actual dread whenever his phone screen lit up and he saw that it was Sam. Yes, Sam was a sacred friend in so many ways: he was often able to receive Johnny without judgment; he was walking the path of liberation; he was in touch with the darkness and grief inside himself. He knew all Johnny's secrets and had never used them against him. But too often, he still met Johnny with cruelty.

Honestly, in my life and in my work, observing my own and others' relationships, I think this is the difficult reality most of us face: more often than not, it's *not* the people we dislike, distrust, or even hate that we struggle with when it comes to being triggered; it's those we like, trust, and love. It's even those we consider sacred friends. And it's these relationships that we tend to keep at even after it would probably serve us both to separate, at least for some time. Albert Einstein said, "Peace cannot be kept by force. It can only be achieved by understanding."[2] While the impulse to keep working on a relationship can be good, sometimes we're simply refusing to accept the reality that what's broken can't be fixed—at least by force. We can't always will our way toward peace; we can't muscle our way to resolution. The idea that resolution is even possible or that it is something we should seek is a form of grasping, a need to hold on. We need to be able to rest in uncertainty and allow the karmic winds to lead.

We hold on so tightly, though, because we fear what we'll lose in letting go. But being a sacred friend also means knowing when to end a relationship. Radical love is a form of labor, after all, and sometimes the work of serving a relationship is saying, "I love you, and I accept you, and the way I feel when we're together is not good for me." You're not canceling them or saying they're a bad person. Though we should be cautious about jumping to cut people from our lives, sacred friendship doesn't mean you have to accept being harmed. It's okay to end a friendship. Radical love does not mean granting someone a free pass to continue to hurt you, themselves, or others.

The question is, how do you know when it's time to end a friendship—in other words, how do you know you're not engaging in spiritual bypassing and a desire to avoid discomfort? And once you do end it, what do you do with your relationship to that person? That might sound counterintuitive; after all, the relationship is over, right? It doesn't exist. But a relationship is something created between two people. It has a life of its own. You may stop having an active cocreated relationship, but all the energy, thought, love, time, and sorrow that unfolded between you doesn't just vaporize once you stop engaging. It lives within you. Your thoughts, feelings, and awareness of the person don't suddenly cease because they're not in front of you.

If you've reached a place where you're aware of a repeating pattern in your friendship and the relationship brings you ongoing pain, it's clear that something is stuck. For whatever reason, one or both of you is unable at this moment to break the pattern. In deciding whether you should stick with it and attempt to disrupt the cycle or walk away, bring it back to the garden. A healthy relationship should function so that both people actively support each other's desire to be happy and to alleviate their suffering. So ask yourself, "Is my friend watering the seeds of love, compassion, and wisdom inside me? Or are they actively watering the seeds of despair, hopelessness, guilt, shame, blame, anger, and resentment inside me?" Only you can answer this question, but the fact that you've arrived at this crossroads signals that the friendship—or this phase of it, at least—has likely run its course. The garden of your inner world is no longer congruent with their gardening skills.

At this point, your responsibility is to take care of your garden, deeply care for it, attend to your triggers, and surrender the relationship to the universe. In Johnny's case, he stopped focusing on Sam and stopped letting him be a weather system that dictated how much peace he felt. This meant he also spent less time in negative thoughts labeling Sam as "damaged," "delusional," and "oblivious." Instead, he turned toward his own feelings of worthlessness, his own need to be special, his drive to feel "chosen." When thoughts of Sam arose, which they did—all the time—instead of engaging with the thoughts, he observed them as they passed and did his best to send him love and compassion. He didn't talk back to the cruelty or engage in arguments with Sam in his mind. Instead, he attended to his feelings, welcoming them with patient kindness, remembering that when big stories arise in the mind, it's a signal that there are big feelings in the body that need our attention. It wasn't that Johnny put Sam "out of mind" but that he loosened his grip, internally, on any outcome for the relationship—he surrendered it to the universe.

Surrendering a situation to the universe, to God, to the holy or divine, to the source, to karma, means surrendering your thoughts about it, surrendering your script. It's realizing that how you've been seeing that person hasn't worked, has not brought repair, has not brought peace, has only brought more inner violence, more inner chaos. When you do end a challenging relationship, or even when you are in the midst of a relationship with a difficult person, it's one of the most transformative actions you can take.

Practice: Give It to the Altar to Be Altered

The political activist, author, and spiritual teacher Marianne Williamson wrote, "I surrender my fears and burdens to God. . . . I know that they will be lifted from me, for what I place on the altar in my mind is then altered in my life."[3] Religions and spiritual practices across the world have used and do use altars as part of their most profound rituals—they are the site where the human and divine meet, where we enact our devotion, where we place our worldly offerings and give them up to something greater than ourselves. Obviously, Marianne Williamson is talking about a metaphorical altar here, but literal altar work is a beautiful instrument for surrender; an altar is a physical site that can simultaneously ground the abstract (our thoughts, feelings, fears, hopes, and intentions) and elevate them beyond the realm of the earthly. If you are at a juncture where you need to surrender a relationship to the universe, I encourage you to try making an altar at home—and place your difficult person (or people) on it. When you place someone on your altar, you're asking for change, for *alteration*, in two ways: you're asking to see them differently, and you're actively wishing them to be at peace so that they show up in the world in a different way.

Creating a Home Altar

1. Dedicate a Space: The English word "altar" derives from a combination of two Latin words: *adolere*, which means "to ritually burn or sacrifice," and *altarium*, meaning "high." The altar elevates. Enter any church, temple, or even home where altars are in use, and you'll see that they are always a raised surface. So in your own home, you'll want to find a raised surface you can dedicate as your altar. This doesn't have to be fancy—it can be a corner of your dresser, a shelf, a small table, or even a kitchen counter. What matters is that this is a dedicated space (i.e., this is its only purpose), one you will see and interact with regularly and that you can keep free of clutter and debris. If you're feeling extra,

you can consider things like the direction the altar faces: maybe you want it to face east, toward the rising sun, or west, toward the setting sun. Maybe you want it to face the direction of your homeland or your ancestors' homeland. If you're in the northern hemisphere, you might want to orient toward Polaris, the North Star, to help keep in mind your own "North Star"—that which guides your movement through the world.

2. Set Your Altar: Gather the objects you'll place on your altar. Keep in mind that the altar is your place to connect with the holy, whatever that means to you. It's your place to connect with mystery, with those forces greater than ourselves, with the people who have come before us and the life that has flowed unbroken through them to us. And, of course, what follows are suggestions only, not hard-and-fast dictates, and the categories may overlap for you.

   • Something that makes you feel at peace and connected to the holy—this could be any combination of photographs of your ancestors, representations of your culture, or personal mementos like a piece of jewelry, personal talismans, or deity representations.

   • Something natural—flowers, river rocks, crystals, leaves, pinecones, beach glass, driftwood, shells; something earthy, you know? Bonus points if it is from or relates to a place or places meaningful to you.

   • Candles or incense—remember the other root of "altar," *adolere*, to ritually burn or sacrifice? Fire can destroy, consume, but it can also purify. It is release, cleansing, new beginnings. It is warmth, heat, light.

3. Place the Difficult Person on the Altar: Write their name on a piece of paper and fold the paper or place it in an envelope. This could be as simple as writing it down on a

slip of notebook paper and folding it in half, or on a piece of that expensive stationery you bought because it made you feel "grown up" but you've never used, or even on the back of a postcard from the city or the school where you met, from the vacation you took together or the one you meant to take but never did. Let your heart lead you. There's no wrong way. Light your candle or incense (for safety, extinguish after you're done with this step), and set the paper with their name on the altar. To yourself, aloud or silently, you can recite, *I surrender, I surrender, I surrender.* Or you could say something like, "Dear Universe, dear God, dear Buddhas, dear Celestial Beings, dear Unseen Forces, help me see what I can't see. Help me change my perspective about this person. Grant them peace." Take some deep breaths and try to find the tension in your body and be with it until you notice it change or pass. Remember, altars are places of sacrifice — we give up something we value (our need to be right, our defense mechanisms, our control) for something else we know is worthier (peace, connection, freedom).

Use your altar as a place to set intentions, connect with your ancestors or holy beings, meditate, pray, do rituals. Just care for it—keep it clean, and occasionally add to it or switch items out as feels right to you. You can pray for your difficult people if you'd like, but you don't need to—you've already surrendered your control over the situation. (I do pray for the difficult folks in my life as part of my practice, and it helps me connect to them at the heart level; it helps me see their humanity.) When it comes to the actual paper with the name of the difficult person on it, leave it be. Let the universe handle it.

Eventually, you'll know when you can remove their name from your altar. When that person surfaces in your mind and you no longer have an intense reaction; when you're no longer engaging with them in your mind, fighting with yourself in your mind about what happened;

when the thought surfaces and it passes, and there is no emotional residue in the body—that's when you know that the work is working; that's when you know that you're starting to get free, when you've learned the karmic lesson on offer.

But only you can know when you've learned the lesson. Only you know if you've cultivated more patience, if you have "graduated." Some people and some situations may heal over time. Perhaps you'll be ready to have that person in your life again after a few years—whatever you need. The point is, you will know when that time is, and it's not necessary to be rigid in this thinking. Remember, this is about learning a lesson and not about punishing the other person. You gave this person/situation to the altar so it could be altered, not so you could win.

You will inevitably be faced with more lessons in different ways and through different people. That is the meaning of life: to continually graduate through life. Difficult people are like messengers, delivering to us things we need to work on. I can't stress this enough. Challenges in all forms are opportunities to see ourselves better, to practice the skills that will lead us to beneficial karma, toward the lives we want. This includes difficult people. Don't blame the messenger. Sometimes we're able to interpret the message only with some perspective. This is where healthy boundaries come into play and are beneficial. And sometimes with perspective, wisdom arises about ourselves—*am I difficult, am I too rigid, am I too fragile?*

But eventually, we do have to revisit that relationship. We have to make peace with the past in order to test the depth of our presence. That's the dance. We're living in a moment when a lot of people are waking up to the idea that some of the dynamics they've normalized in their lives are not, in fact, acceptable. There's a lot of chatter swirling around about narcissistic parents, going no contact, and the like. And to a degree, *yes.* To a degree, that's great. The problem is, people will go ten, fifteen, twenty years without speaking to multiple people in their lives. They feel like if they avoid and neglect and reject and push away, don't see and don't engage, they're becoming free. But our freedom is truly actualized only in context with the other.

It's one thing to protect your peace. Sometimes you've got to take yourself out of the equation for a while to care for yourself so you can be more confident, more energized. But that's not spirituality—that's personal development. Ask yourself: now that you have "protected your peace" and are presumably operating from a place of greater equanimity, of greater serenity, can you sustain it outside your bubble? Can you drive down the hill and wait in that line and miss your train and deal respectfully with that colleague, that shop assistant, that nurse who reminds you of your father, your sister, your ex-best friend? Because you're going to have to. The spiritual path will always push us back into the fire. It will naturally bring back the past so it, so we, can be transformed. So you can have a moment of transfiguration when the burdensome way you saw a person or experience no longer triggers you.

Bamboo, Not Barbed Wire

One of the most common ways we try to avoid our triggers is by erecting iron-clad boundaries around ourselves, impenetrable fortresses that make us *feel* safe but that in actuality isolate us, broadcasting to the world that we're not accessible, we're not relatable, we're someone to avoid. We also tend to use boundaries as emotional suits of armor, protecting our future selves from past hurts—"I was abandoned by someone I thought was a close friend" becomes "I don't let people get close" energy. Again, you send the message that you are someone to avoid, someone who doesn't want to be known. In the name of protection, you actually ward off love and connection—the *opposite* of what you want. We all remember quarantine, right? Sheltering in place is *supposed* to be an emergency response.

Not every trigger, not every social pain, is an emergency. But we've become accustomed to treating them as if they are, accustomed to normalizing hysteria. We've also started treating boundaries—or the crossing of them—as an unpardonable offense without examining the boundaries themselves or our responsibility for enforcing them. We're going from "You crossed a boundary" to "See you never." This is some Alice in Wonderland mirror-world shit, honey—healthy boundaries don't separate you from other people. When we have healthy boundaries, we communicate clearly what we need and expect from others. Healthy boundaries generate respect and understanding, which bring you closer together. If your boundaries aren't supporting your liberation? Then, sis, you have some serious checking in to do with yourself.

Let's just take it back to basics here, embrace being a beginner. What is a boundary, literally? Like, in real life? It's what separates one place from another, right? It's the line in the sand, the border, the river, the limit where one thing ends and another begins. Applying that metaphorically, to a person or a boundary, then, is where *you* end and *I* begin. It's the line you draw between what you will allow and what you will not. It's training your understanding that you can only ever control your own behavior—you set boundaries for *yourself*, not others. This is where so many of us lose the plot. We think setting boundaries is all about dictating the behavior of others. No, baby. People do what they're gonna do. When we set boundaries, we are clear about what we own and what we do not, such as responsibility for how other people act, what they think, or how they feel. When we set boundaries, we make room for ourselves—a space other people aren't constantly intruding upon—in which we can honestly assess what we care about and how we want to relate to others. A boundary creates healthy distance; it creates perspective.

To be fair, we don't get a ton of training setting healthy boundaries growing up. Most of us learn to have either boundaries that are too weak or boundaries that are too rigid. Weak boundaries are porous—the "separation" between yourself and another is blurry, there's a lot of people pleasing, there's a lot of fear of rejection, there's a lot of resentment. Rigid boundaries are inflexible defense mechanisms, and there's a lot of fear of being hurt. It's the inflexible kind that we're mostly talking about here—though porous boundaries are also harmful to genuine sacred friendship (oh, but don't you worry, we will be talking about them in the next chapter)—because they're so often used as an excuse to ignore your own work. These are boundaries as trauma responses, boundaries as control, boundaries born of hysteria, boundaries based on avoidance of challenging emotions. When used this way, boundaries are a form of spiritual bypassing, similar to canceling someone or cutting them out of your life entirely.

The irony is, those who are the most invested in activism or personal growth or loudest about walking the path of liberation are often the ones with the most rigid boundaries. There's a kind of "true believer" energy to rigid boundaries, an attitude of "things must be done this way or else." That's zealotry. Overly rigid boundaries come into play in a variety of scenarios. First and foremost, the one we've been talking about, and why we're here: you're quick to cut people out of your life or you've repeatedly cut meaningful people from your life. But also, you might have rigid boundaries if apologies mean little to you. You don't take other people's views into consideration, you don't consider the input of others. You take criticism really personally (rigid boundaries are a shield against that). You have strict rules about what you do and when, which you are unwilling to ever bend for others; you have strict rules about what others do and how they can be in relationship with you—when they can call, text, how often, etc., with little to no room for grace.

Being able to communicate your limits and your limitations is very healthy, especially for meaningful connection. You should be able to tell your friend or your partner or your roommates, "Hey, I need quiet time to myself every day" and not feel guilty for expressing that. Yes, if someone knocks on your door five minutes after you told them you needed to be alone, they are crossing a boundary. But are you immediately jumping all over them for it (outwardly or inwardly), or are you willing to take a beat and see why? Rather than concrete topped with barbed wire, boundaries should be made of bamboo—strong and durable but with some softness, flexibility, bending in the wind as life requires. If your boundaries are super-rigid, ask yourself, are they really helping you or hurting you? It's fine to say no often, but only if you know how to say yes just as frequently. You should allow your boundaries to change as you change.

We all have many different types of boundaries—emotional, physical, material, intellectual, time-based—and how important they are to us and where we've marked their limits will vary from person to person and context to context. The key to those boundaries being healthy, to having good boundaries, is knowing what you want from a given relationship and having a clear grasp on your values. When we don't have a strong sense of what we value, when we aren't clear on what we believe when it comes to how to treat others, how we want to be treated, and how we believe we should show up in the world, it's hard to set boundaries.

If you live by your values, you live with integrity, and when you live with integrity, you know your boundaries (and when they're crossed). That's actually when "healthy" conflict arises—yes, conflict is neutral, but here I mean it arises from a healthy place, one that is self-aware rather than reactive. Unfortunately, most people have no fucking idea what they value. And because they don't know what they value, they don't live with integrity, and because they don't live with integrity, their boundaries are constantly in motion and therefore constantly crossed so that any minor thing could be blown out of proportion.

Inevitably, in setting boundaries, you will encounter people who respond poorly to them. There are a lot of overgrown five-year-olds out there who don't like hearing "No." But when your boundaries are healthy, this won't be a disaster. It won't be an emergency, because you'll be steady in your conviction; you won't second-guess yourself, because your boundary supports you living in integrity with what you value. And when you encounter someone else's boundary, rather than being offended, you'll understand that it is an expression of their needs, not a judgment of you or an attempt to control your behavior. When you have good boundaries, you are proactive, not *reactive*. When you have rigid boundaries, you're always *reacting*. In a way, it's not about you. You're constantly oriented toward other people's behaviors, creating a fortress around yourself based on your triggers. Growth and connection cannot happen under these conditions. Boundaries should be created and laid out as points of knowing, of restoration, of repair, of well-being, of understanding how far you can stretch before you have to rest.

Use boundaries to honor and reinforce the respectful and loving behavior you deserve from others, to increase your well-being, not to hide from life.

Practice: Boundaries for Life

Setting healthy boundaries in our relationships is critical to real connection. When we have healthy boundaries—boundaries that are neither too porous nor too rigid—the people we care about understand our needs more clearly, as well as how to meet them.

Showing people what we need can feel deeply uncomfortable, though—it can feel *vulnerable*. Ironically, even though a boundary indicates a limit, an uncrossable line, and therefore a safe or appropriate distance between us and another person, setting a boundary can make us feel *open* to being wounded. It's normal to feel that way. We can feel vulnerable when we set boundaries with people in our lives because we're afraid of how they'll respond to those boundaries. We fear they'll be angry, or hurt, or disapproving. We fear being rejected—losing that person, losing that connection, losing that belonging.

As hard as it is, we need to remind ourselves that setting boundaries is an act of radical love and compassion that serves both of us. When we set a boundary, we acknowledge that which we deserve unconditionally. The boundary isn't premised on our behavior, but it also isn't premised on the behavior of the other person. When we set a boundary, we acknowledge what causes us suffering and seek to alleviate it. In doing so, we also seek to alleviate the suffering of another person by diminishing the possibility of unnecessary conflict between us.

Maintaining healthy boundaries is a three-part process. In order to set boundaries, you have to *determine* what your boundaries are. Once you know what your boundaries are, you need to *communicate* them. And finally, you have to *hold* them. Setting boundaries is ongoing work unique to every relationship. What follows is a loose guide for considering boundaries in individual relationships, not necessarily a template for creating a set of boundaries you apply across your life.

Determine: In order to set a boundary, you have to know what the boundary is. Since boundaries may vary from relationship to relationship (and context to context), it's important to consider what your needs are in any given relationship. Perhaps, for example, you have an older sibling you really look up to. You realize one of your needs in this relationship is respect. Whatever they may be, take time to write these needs down. Now, consider your values. Lucky for you, you've done this work (or a good chunk of it) already in chapter 2. Pull up the list you put together as you answered those questions about whom you admire, what you want, what inspires you, what fulfills you. Now, ask yourself two questions: "Does this relationship meet or fail to meet my needs?" and "In this relationship, am I able to be in integrity with my values?" Your answers to these questions can point the way to where you need to set better boundaries. For example, you may realize that your older sibling, who constantly criticizes your choices such as where you work, where you live, and whom you date—does not meet your need for respect.

Communicate: People are not mind readers. The point of a boundary is to bolster relationships, not quit them. The idea is not to set a boundary in your head and then cancel someone for violating it. It's on you to let your sibling, for example, know what your boundary is—ideally before they have a chance to cross it. Be calm, direct, and unhesitating. Focus on yourself and refrain from making accusations. Remember, this isn't about them—you're not here to control them or punish them. So, bringing it back to your imaginary sibling, you might say, "It's really important to me to feel respected. Second-guessing my career choices feels disrespectful to me. That's not a conversation I'm open to having." What you wouldn't say is, "When you second-guess my career choices, you're being disrespectful. If you do that again, I'm leaving." The focus is on what you do, not telling the other person what not to do.

Hold: Boundaries work only if you hold them. Say your sibling did, indeed, bring up your work after all. You might say, "I'm not interested in talking about this now." If they persist and you're with them in person, you could respectfully say, "Thank you for meeting me for coffee/lunch/drinks. It means a lot to me. I'm going to head home now. Take care/be safe." If you're on the phone, same thing: "Good talking to you. I love you. I'm going to go now." You don't need to justify or explain your boundary. You don't need to defend it. And you definitely don't need to argue and shouldn't get sucked into an argument about it. When you continue to engage with a person who doesn't respect your boundaries, you're sending the message that perhaps there's some validity in second-guessing you. There isn't. Part of holding your boundaries successfully is preparing yourself for this possibility or, worse, more negative outcomes, such as anger-based responses. Remember that their response reflects only on them, not you.

Chapter 5

Staying in the Fire

Conflict is a kind of crucible if we can stay in the fire long enough to be transformed. When we stay in the fire, when we tolerate—even welcome—difficult feelings rather than shut down or run away, we have this incredibly profound opportunity to forge even deeper bonds in relationship. In conflict, we can come to learn what really matters to a person, what their needs are, what they're longing for. We develop emotional intimacy and strengthen our ability to view life beyond the confines of our own limited perspective. If we dip out every time we encounter conflict, hardship, or disagreement, however, we pretty much ensure that our relationships stay at surface level. Over time, we also train our friends, our family, our lovers not to be honest with us, not to trust us with their pain, not to address anything that might spark conflict, because what would be the point? We've successfully taught everyone around us, as well as ourselves, that we don't have the capacity to deal with hard things. Worse, we've taught ourselves that we are *entitled* to only "good" feelings.

But even when we *think* we're willing to stay in the fire, even when we show up for conflict—when we attend to our triggers and don't use boundaries as emotional armor—it can be so intensely uncomfortable that it feels almost impossible to stay present. Tolerating emotional discomfort, being able to sit with difficult feelings, is a huge part of walking the path of liberation. Intense feelings manifest in the same way—in the body—whether we are alone or with another person. And yet when we are with another person, the intensity of those feelings can seem dialed up. Just being with those feelings, allowing them to move through you and staying centered, is so much harder.

Why? When you're with another person, there's an energetic exchange. There's body language to contend with, facial expressions, eye contact; there are layers upon layers of communication to process beyond what's being said. Even normally, when we're not in conflict, many nonverbal cues are constantly being processed between two people face-to-face. Now, imagine all that amplified by what feels like super-high-stakes emotions. With the amount of signals to process, it becomes almost impossible to rest in your center. It's unquestionably harder to rest in the present when you're emotionally activated and relating to another person.

When this is going on, it's easier to buy in to the conditioning that "They made me feel this way." It's easier to give up responsibility for what's going on in your body. It's easier to believe those feelings are the truth about the moment, are the truth about who you are, are the truth about who that person is. Difficult emotions in the context of conflict are seductive in a way, because they reinforce the conditioning that the self we cherish so much exists entirely outside the social body, outside a collective context—that we are separate from each other.

Having the capacity to be in your center even when your body is flooded with emotions, even when your mind is flooded with destructive narratives, takes a lot of skill. This is where doing the work between you and you—that first half of the liberation equation—comes in. You have to regularly practice being in your body, being with your feelings, coming back to center when you're *alone* in order to have any hope of doing so with another person present. You need to commit yourself to the practices of sitting with hard feelings (as in chapter 2) and observation without evaluation (as in chapter 3). Having a daily centering practice makes it possible to observe the chaos that's happening inside your body, inside your mind, and that is spilling from the other person without getting carried away, without evaluating what you observe. It's really, really fucking hard. But it is possible.

The goal of staying in the fire is not to be *consumed* by it, right? We don't want to be consumed by our feelings. It's important to remember that some feelings can have more of an inflammatory texture than others, especially when experienced repeatedly without access to your center. But it's how we relate to those feelings that creates rigidity and contraction within us. Even if we're far from having mastered a practice of returning to or staying in our bodies at times of heightened emotion, there is always something available to us, something we can all do, at any time, on the fly, to at least momentarily disrupt our reactivity: connect to our breath.

Practice: Connect to the Breath

When you're hit with an intense emotion, it can be a major struggle just to stay present, let alone process the feeling in the body. No matter how intense things get, though, your breath is always there for you. Even when you find yourself activated and reactive, you can still connect to your breath. What's so great about taking a breath?

Breath keeps us present. Breath is the gateway to the present moment. If we're hooked and looping in the past, or future-tripping, it's nearly impossible to meet a moment of conflict with maturity, let alone radical love and compassion. The present is the place of possibility. In life, but especially in conflict, we tend to focus on desired outcomes—in other words, we focus on the future, and a very specific future at that. Our view of what *could be* becomes very limited. We believe that we can be happy only if we get exactly what we want. That's the mentality of an addict: *I need this in order to feel that.*

Breath grounds us in the body. When you invite in a breath, you give your mind the coordinates of your body. Focusing on the sensation of breathing immediately grounds you in your physical being. Being in the body is critical to being present. As we've said before— where does the body live? In the present.

Breath creates calm. Breath not only grounds you in the body, it also regulates the body. Controlled breathing can slow your heart rate, lower your blood pressure, and activate the parasympathetic nervous system, signaling the sympathetic nervous system that it doesn't need to fight, flee, or freeze. It's incredibly difficult to concentrate and bring focused present-moment awareness to conflict when your nervous system is going haywire.

Breath creates space. Taking a breath creates a pause between emotion and response. It creates space between feeling and narrative. In that space, we have room to recognize our emotions, opportunity to name them. Doing so is an act of observation that helps us to create separation (space) between the feeling and the self. It's in these spaces that wisdom often emerges, that we hear spirit whispering.

How to Connect to Your Breath

Place both hands on your belly. Slowly inhale through your nose, counting to four. As you inhale, imagine that you are pulling the breath in and down, filling your belly and lifting your hands. Keep your shoulders relaxed. Exhale through your nose, counting to four. Hold the emptiness for four.

Now, scan your body for any tension. If you locate tension, rest your attention there for a bit and offer these words to that sensation: "Hello, friend. You are welcome here."

Remember to not entertain the stories that are entangled with the tension and to just focus on the feeling in the body for what it is: **a passing sensation.**

Hold Loosely to Your Strategy and Firmly to Your Needs

Remember our old friends the shoelace and the snake? The shoelace is a feeling, and feelings live in the body. The snake is the mind's perception of the shoelace—it is our meaning-making machine's *response* to the feeling. The snake is a story, and a story that arises from the past (that superscary time you were bitten by a snake). When we practice sitting with that uncomfortable feeling long enough—say, fear—we gradually come to see that there is no snake. Our perception changes.

I bring this up as a reminder that in conflict, as well, our minds respond to big feelings in the body with even bigger stories about what's happening in the present moment. And to then underscore that, nine times out of ten, these stories are not a reflection of what's happening in front of us. They are stories we've been hauling along with us from the past into the present, old emotional baggage that we drag with us into every meaningful or fraught interaction. We then let the story attached to the initial feeling of discomfort steal the show completely. We react *to the story*, not to what the other person is saying or doing per se—and we react in the same harmful and hurtful ways that we always have. Our reaction is also a kind of script, one we've memorized by adulthood.

When we stay in the fire, however, we move past the past into the present. The fire eventually burns itself out. We learn that the feelings pass if we let them. And we can finally stop reacting automatically, finally drop that script. In the aftermath of the fire, on the other side of the intense feelings, our perception changes; we are open to seeing ourselves and each other differently—to listening and hearing each other with *awareness* and thus *compassion*.

When we're in conflict and operating from our shadows, letting our stories run the show, the chances that we'll come to a mutual understanding are slim to fucking none—because we don't understand why we're really clashing in the first place. We don't have *self-awareness*, let alone awareness of another person's interiority, their emotional landscape, their reality. Without awareness, there is no compassion.

Interpersonal conflict can emerge from competing values, motivations, desires, ideas, judgments, misinformation, or misunderstanding, *but* underneath the outline of whatever particular conflict is unfolding is the same core issue: getting our needs met. This is the basic premise of Nonviolent Communication (or NVC, as I'll call it from here out): that every action we take is an attempt to meet a need, and nowhere is this truer than in conflict. When we're *aware* of this—as we have room to be if we can stay in the fire—it becomes easier to understand our own and each other's choices, behaviors, and actions—and to move away from shame, blame, finger pointing, assignment of "right" and "wrong," identifying ourselves or others as "good" or "bad," and the desire for retribution or punishment. All those things that add pain to what is already painful . . . or that we might call "violent." In other words, all those things that create *suffering*.

NVC is a lot of things—you could describe it as a tool, as a process, as a system, but I think it's simplest to say that at its heart, it's a philosophy of being, a model for how to be *with each other* in the world. Marshall Rosenberg, the founder of NVC, described it as based on the principle of *ahimsa*,[1] an ethic shared by Buddhism, Hinduism, and Jainism that directs us to live in such a way that we cause no harm to any living being, including ourselves, in thought, speech, or action. In this way, you can see ahimsa as an extension of compassion: our desire to alleviate suffering means that we also commit to not causing it. As His Holiness the Dalai Lama said, "The true expression of nonviolence is compassion."[2]

When we're aware that we're all just trying to get our needs met, we're empowered to transform judgment into compassion. We have empathy for each other's suffering—in this case, the pain of an unmet need—and a desire to alleviate it. Compassion helps us to stay present—it helps us to focus on understanding ourselves and each other rather than reaching for blame-centered stories (turning toward the past) or outcomes (turning toward the future). And being present helps us to remain compassionate: when we're truly present, we listen to the words being said without getting dragged into new storylines in our mind, and we listen to the spaces between the words, where wisdom so often emerges.

In sacred friendship, listening like this is like an act of devotion, because it allows us to truly see—and be seen by—others, to experience belonging. As Kristin Masters, a longtime practitioner of NVC and certified NVC trainer, beautifully described it in a conversation with me, "If we know how to actually hear what somebody is saying, if we know how to hear what they're *longing for*, instead of hearing the chatter, then we have the opportunity to really know each other and be known—to take risks and be real with each other—without sacrificing our belonging, the ultimate human need."[3]

I love Kristin's focus on longing here, because it goes so directly to the heart of what it is to be human. In Kristin's experience working with everyone from incarcerated people to students training in NVC, the word "need" triggers the shadow in most people. Because the first step in communicating well in conflict is self-awareness, it seems natural to try to identify our own needs, right? But Kristin suggests instead that, in moments of conflict, we try asking ourselves, "What I am longing for? What am I dreaming of?" When we know the answers to those questions, when we can pay attention to our motivations, then we can figure out how to move in that direction, how to ask for that need to be met. The same goes for listening to others: rather than listen to the complaint, listen to the dream. That's our path toward meeting their need.

In NVC, the ask or request to have a need met is called a "strategy." Whatever action we think can be taken to meet a need is a type of strategy: "I want you to call me every day" and "I am going to make an effort to say 'yes' to more invitations" are both strategies to meet a need for connection, for example. This doesn't mean both strategies are equally likely to be successful. But when we have clarity about what we're really seeking, what we're longing for, we can be better informed about choosing a strategy to get there. I have a lot more control over saying yes than I do over when you decide to pick up the phone. The thing is, there are almost always many strategies available to us, but as humans, we tend to get very tightfisted and unmoving about the "right" way a need "should" be met. Our strategies become very narrow when our understanding is narrow—we tell ourselves, "The only way for me to feel secure is if I am the most important person to my friend/ family member/lover and they prove that by sending me my favorite flowers/framing a photo of us in their home/etc." In reality, there are lots of ways for you to meet your need for security: some of them may be internal, some may be relational, some will come from the world. And some will emerge from that layer of simply knowing and affirming that you matter, that your need matters, and that it will continue to matter whether it is met or not, because in life, not everything is going to work out, and not every need will be met in every relationship or dynamic. Even if we can't meet them, we still get to acknowledge that they're there.

As Kristin beautifully says, "We want to hold loosely to our strategies and firmly to our needs." We need to acknowledge our needs, and the needs of others, and love them rather than shrink from them. We need each other, after all. Underneath our conditioning, we share the same core needs: the need to belong, the need to feel known and accepted, the need to matter, the need to feel safe. Understanding this reveals that what we have in common far outweighs our differences, which creates connection. When we can put that all out on the table—in conflict or in building friendships—when we can bring a warm curiosity to each other's experience without insisting on some "right way" of meeting a need, we have so much creative intelligence available to us. Together, we can often find a strategy that works for both of us or, as sometimes happens, acknowledge that it's not going to work anymore. When we focus on needs instead of blame or judgment, we are freed from our habit of figuring out who's wrong, who has a problem, who should suffer, and how many other people should suffer.

Instead we foster empathy, for ourselves as well as others, and connection. We get to experience the joy of giving and receiving radical love. Instead of operating on autopilot, we're better able to stabilize our present-moment awareness, to be in the here and now, to remain rooted in our bodies and respond from that grounded space. We affirm that the answer to one of our deepest fears—do I matter?—is *yes*.

Practice: NVC for Beginners

Learning and practicing NVC is like learning a new language. It requires ongoing practice to become fluent in it, and even after years of speaking it, you'll still make the mistakes of a non-native speaker and discover nuances you hadn't realized were there before. I say all this not only to encourage you to seek out more resources about NVC but to emphasize that what follows is a very basic representation of NVC, designed to introduce you to its fundamental concepts and stretch your muscles.

As a process, NVC combines four components—observation, feelings, needs, and requests—with two parts: honesty and empathy. The two aims are, one, to clearly express how "I am" without blaming or criticizing others—in other words, to be honest about your state of being without locating responsibility for it in others. And two, to receive with empathy how "you are" without hearing blame or criticism—in other words, to listen to someone else's expression of their state of being without taking it as a personal attack.

The Four Components

1. Observation: This is where you get to use your observation-without-evaluation muscles. In NVC, observation means taking notice of concrete actions and the environment around us without interpretation or judgment. For example, "I noticed that when you sat down at our table, you said hello to everyone but me" is a neutral observation of an action, as opposed to "When you came to the table, you ignored me and made a show of greeting everyone else."

2. Feelings: What we observe is likely to elicit a feeling within us. Here, we want to identify the feeling while separating it from our thoughts. This is where we get to practice our skill in *drop the story, deal with the feeling*. For example, you might say, "When I noticed you said hello to everyone but me, I felt embarrassed and hurt" as opposed to, "When you came in and ignored me, you made it obvious you don't care about me." Rather than interpreting the other person's action and making assumptions about their inner life, you remain focused on the experience and sensations of your own life.

3. Needs: In NVC, feelings are a result of a met or unmet need. Our feeling may be related to an action (not being greeted), but it is not caused by the action—it arises from the need (in

this case, the unmet need). So we need to focus on what the feeling signals—identifying what need is going unmet. It's really important here to separate needs from strategies. "I need you to acknowledge me" is actually a strategy. Anytime we include a person, place, location, time, or object in identification of a need, what we're really describing is a strategy. Instead, try to focus on language that describes universal human needs. The feeling of embarrassment at not being greeted may signal an unmet need for respect. The feeling of hurt may signal an unmet need for mutual recognition, for knowing that you matter to that person as much as they matter to you. When you focus on your needs and really home in on them, you are better equipped to make meaningful requests and less likely to become attached to one strategy.

4. Requests: Once we've identified our need, we usually have a few strategies in mind to meet that need. A request is when we ask someone to cooperate with us in executing that strategy. Requests are different from demands—there is an implied "must" in a demand: "You must do this for me to feel that." One way to check whether you're requesting or demanding is to ask yourself if you're willing to hear "No." If you're not, your "request" is likely a demand. Requests should be respectful, clear, and doable. The best way to achieve this is for them to be specific and measurable and to identify your need. Focus on positive language—expressing what you would like someone to do rather than on what you don't want them to do. In our dinner-party scenario, you might say something like, "I would appreciate it if you would greet me when you join our group. It's important to me to be acknowledged as part of our friend circle, and I think that would prevent misunderstanding between us."

A "cheat sheet" of the NVC model (I mean, you could literally write this down and keep it on your phone) might look like this:

When I see _____

I feel _____

Because my need for _____ is/isn't being met

Would you be willing to _____?

You can flip this model to connect empathetically with another person by trying to suss out their feelings and needs. Much as we discussed in our practice of emotional validation, communicating to another person that you understand their feelings and needs doesn't mean agreeing to act in a way that doesn't meet your own needs. Instead, you are validating that they matter and expressing a desire to find a strategy that will work for both of you. To do so, reverse the previous four statements and transform them into questions as needed, keeping in mind that the other person is the ultimate authority on their experience:

When you see _____

Do you feel _____?

Because your need for _____ is/isn't being met?

Would you like _____?

Restoring Goodness

As we touched on, part of the beauty of NVC is how it frees us from our habit of figuring out who's wrong, who has a problem, who should suffer, and how many other people should suffer. These strategies are the essence of a punitive mindset, a worldview based on the premise that undesirable behaviors can only be prevented or corrected through punishment. Seen through this lens, when a person commits a wrong (or a perceived wrong) they are required to suffer in return for what they did; the focus is punishing their "badness" rather than restoring their goodness.

The punitive mindset is deeply embedded in all our psyches—because it's the very air we breathe. It is the basis of the American judicial system. In the U.S., there are many states where there are more people incarcerated than living on college campuses, and we spend more on incarceration than we do public education. Capital punishment is legal in 27 states. Punitive thinking is built into the DNA of our society—and it emerges from that same mistake in perception that leads us to identify our behaviors and actions with the process we call the self. We *also* identify the behaviors of *others* as indistinct from who they are as a person. A person who does something bad is "a bad person." There can only be the possibility that they might one day be worthy again of connection, worthy of friendship and worthy of respect, if "they pay for what they did."

This is how relationships fall apart. This is how we remain isolated, because we're "right" and they're wrong; we're "good" and they're "bad." So dismantling the punitive mindset within, especially when it comes to resolving conflict, is critical to practicing authentic connection. I mean, just think about a time you were punished for a mistake you made in a relationship. Ask yourself—did it restore your goodness? Did it transform the relationship for the better, or were you left hurting and resentful?

Maybe right now you're thinking, "This doesn't apply to me, skip. I don't relish seeing other people suffer for their 'sins.'" Sorry, sis—almost all of us have an "inner punisher." Just because you may not be actively seeking to punish, doesn't mean you're not engaging in punitive behavior. When was the last time you gave someone the silent treatment? When was the last time you withheld affection? In our intimate lives, punishing can often be triggered by jealousy or insecurity. Punishing in these contexts can be as subtle as acting distant toward your friend or partner after they show up late for lunch. Sitting there, waiting for them, you may feel that they don't value your time—or, even worse, you. Once they finally arrive, you intentionally engage only at the bare minimum. That choice to be distant and cold, to not engage, is punishment for what you perceive they did "wrong." So much relationship-based conflict is rooted in punitive thinking.

When you bring awareness to your "inner punisher," you realize that punitive consciousness bleeds in subtle ways into our words, actions, thoughts, and feelings. You may not be a person who punishes others outwardly, but wishing harm on others, fantasizing about revenge, internally judging are all expressions of a punitive mindset, and they carry karmic consequences. By watering the seeds of judgment, self-righteousness, superiority, you actively nurture harmful karma.

Stop chasing harm. Instead of making your life about finding ways to punish people who hurt you (or finding ways to punish yourself), focus instead on the goodness that is always there—your goodness, other peoples' goodness, and community goodness. That is the essence of a restorative approach to conflict. When you are open to this way of thinking, you reinforce your ability to separate the behavior of a person from who the person is at the core of their being. When you remember your goodness and the goodness of others, the fear-based, judgment-based voices quiet down. That's the path of liberation. You are led by your own goodness and attracted to goodness in others.

When someone commits a wrong (real or perceived), we do not need to create more harm by inflicting pain. Instead, we need to rest in our faith in karma. Let go, release your grip on outcomes. Accept that you won't always witness the resolution you longed for. Karma serves each and every single one of us the lessons that we need to learn and to grow. You are ultimately responsible only for your actions; not only is it too daunting to be responsible for everyone else's too, it simply is not your role. You are not God; you are not karma. Have unwavering faith that the world restores itself. I know this is a lot to ask, especially for those of us who have endured a lot of pain at the hands of other people. But when you can release the hold that your anger, resentment, and your past have on you, you can find real freedom.

It's important to be clear here that I'm not advocating you no longer hold people accountable for their actions (which you do by holding and enforcing your own boundaries) or become blissfully ignorant to the realities of life. Responsibility for harm caused is never excused. A restorative approach does not excuse violent, harmful, abusive behavior. We're not talking about being indifferent to injustice here. We are talking about relating to injustice from a place of goodness, however.

When we witness wrongdoing, either firsthand or from a distance, our tendency is to identify a perpetrator and imagine how they should be punished for causing harm. *But our desire to punish doesn't actually change the situation.* All it does is breed destructive thoughts. The thoughts you cultivate, and your ability—or lack of ability—to perceive goodness in others, are essential to your liberation. When you see people making mistakes, your karmic momentum pivots on your response. You can disrupt punitive thought patterns by telling yourself, "Okay, I see that this person is doing something that I believe to be wrong. And I believe they need to take responsibility. *And* I will not let their behavior overshadow my knowing that despite the fact they're currently lost in the soup of chaos, at their core, they are a benevolent being."

You might be thinking, "So you're telling me to do nothing when I see wrongdoing?" No, not at all. I welcome you to be of service and take true action. What do I mean? I mean, take all that energy you're using on judging and punishing and do something real *to restore goodness*: use your platform to share meaningful antiracism resources; advocate for domestic abuse survivors; donate to mental health organizations—there are endless possibilities when it comes to how you can be of help. Use your time to learn about the origins of inequities in your community and identify the skills you have that can combat and repair the situations from which injustices emerge.

Because, in one sense, the most dangerous part of a punitive mindset is how it excuses *us* from our responsibility to create the conditions of liberation not just for ourselves, but for others. A punitive mindset discourages self-awareness. It encourages us to point the finger, to reinforce the delusion of separateness, to keep us incarcerated in the prison of our conditioning. A restorative mindset returns us to self-awareness, to an orientation toward liberation.

When it comes to *how* to hold people accountable for their harmful actions without perpetuating further harm, the truth is that I don't have the perfect answer. I don't think there *is* one right solution. What I do know is that our current system isn't working. Incarceration doesn't actually keep us safe. It doesn't prevent people from committing crimes or reoffending. Instead it traumatizes and retraumatizes prisoners, without changing the factors or environment that enabled their destructive behaviors. The people housed within our prisons often come from communities that carry histories of profound pain and trauma. We have to find other ways to hold people to account—and to prevent the harm in the first place. Freedom is relational—we are not free until we are all free. Warehousing humans in cells, isolating them, hiding them from view, cannot sever the threads that connect us within our collective spiritual tapestry.

What I do know is this: when we embrace a change of heart, even toward those who have wounded us, the path toward the next right action becomes clear. It emerges through presence and forgiveness, echoing the truth that our capacity for change and healing knows no bounds.

Tell the Weather, Don't Be the Weather

NVC is a beautiful framework for practicing self-awareness in conflict. When we are in conflict, when we argue, we're often not aware of our responses, of the why behind how we fight. By bringing awareness to what's really going on—*why* we're fighting—we can change *how* we fight. Instead of fighting, we can communicate *consciously*. We're empowered to pause, and as we gain awareness of how we operate, we can then share that awareness by bringing the other person into our process. This technique of bringing someone else into your process is what Rachel Pringle, my dear friend and intimacy coach, calls "Conscious Communication."[4]

Like NVC, Conscious Communication is a liberatory way of communicating that does away with the winner/loser approach to conflict. Conscious communication frees you to say anything, with love and without blame, no matter how scary. Rachel's method for deepening emotional intimacy—for deepening connection in all relationships—speaks so powerfully to me in part because it exists firmly in the realm of the third truth. Conscious Communication begins with the premise that what we are experiencing at any given moment does not represent the totality of our experience. How we feel in the moment is not the only way we're feeling. What we're thinking represents only one perception of reality. In other words, the way you feel when you are in an argument with someone now isn't the whole truth of who you are, much as the thoughts that populate your mind after feeling an intense emotion are not the whole truth of who you are.

In Conscious Communication, we flex the muscles of our "parts vocabulary" and our radical honesty to literally verbalize to ourselves and to the other person that only *a part* of us (not the whole) feels angry, hurt, upset, etc. Instead of resorting to totalizing our feelings—"I hate you"—we say, "When you act in that way, *a part* of me feels this way. When I feel this, these are the kinds of thoughts that pass my mind." Rejecting feelings as totalizing is really transformative for both parties, as it leaves room for the "and." "I'm angry, *and* I love you." "I'm sad, *and* I want to be close."

To do this, we have to be willing to look at ourselves in parts and to be honest about those parts. We can't be afraid to say, "Hey, when you did that, I felt my abandonment wound activated. And a part of me experienced really disturbing thoughts and challenging feelings. And that leads a part of me to want to say this and this and this, and it leads me to want to do this and this and this."

I like to think of this skill as our ability to tell the weather while remembering that we're not the weather. To tell the weather, not *be* the weather. It's like being able to say, "When this happens, there's a freaking thunderstorm inside me. It's pouring rain. It's hailing and it's cold, all at once. It's a hurricane." You have the space to observe and share what's currently happening in you without mistaking what's happening as the truth of who you are.

Let's look at an example. My student Maya had a really difficult relationship with her mom. She hadn't spoken to her in over a decade, because she couldn't tolerate her mom's judgment of her life and her choices. Maya is a lesbian, she works as a painter, and for years, she has volunteered at a women's correctional facility. For Maya's mom, her sexual identity, her job, and her unwillingness to castigate offenders as irredeemable criminals were not only distasteful but practically immoral.

When she and her mom *were* speaking, her mom would constantly insinuate that her relationship with her girlfriend (now wife) was just a phase and that eventually, she would meet the "right" man and return to the warm embrace of heterosexuality. She demeaned her work, insisting that Maya would never be able to support herself despite the glaring fact that she already supported herself. She belittled the women at the prison where Maya volunteered, emphasizing that they wouldn't be there if they hadn't done something wrong.

Maya had been dealing by avoiding all family get-togethers, blocking her mom on social media, and communicating with her siblings only as necessary. After about ten years of this, her sister let her know her mom was sick. She had written Maya a letter, and her sister asked if she could give it to her. The letter essentially said, "I don't know how much more time I have to live. I really want you back in my life. I love you. Please forgive me, I'm so sorry." Maya found herself torn. She asked herself, "Do I invite her back in? Is it even worth my time?"

In the past, whenever Maya and her mom saw each other, it was painful and hard. Maya always left their interactions angry, and when she felt angry with her mom, the same thoughts always surfaced in her mind: "I hate you; I never want to talk to you again; you're the worst mother in the world; all my problems are because of you." She turned the blame for everything difficult in her life on her mother. She became her mother's victim in her narrative, her thoughts spiraling: "My life sucks because of you. I struggled to find love, because you never gave me the love I needed. I've never known how to create security for myself, because you never made me feel secure. All I owe you is the pain you gave me." She would then react to the stories with self-destructive behaviors like binge drinking and eating. Maya was lost in the blame-victim-punisher soup, adding pain to what was already painful.

In the years since, Maya had pushed herself to embrace parts vocabulary. She decided to speak with her mom and address their dynamic using the tools of Conscious Communication. When she visited her mother, she explained, "Mom, when you tell me that you don't approve of how I live my life, a part of me feels angry. When that part of me feels angry, I believe that you don't love me. I think that you actually are disgusted by me, and when I think these thoughts, I react by pushing you away, and when I push you away, I self-destruct by binge drinking and eating."

This practice takes strength, courage, and vulnerability. But when Maya finally spoke to her mom with that level of intimacy, her mom broke down crying and finally understood her daughter's process and the level of pain it aroused. She apologized sincerely, explaining that she had never known her statements were so impactful to her daughter. Maya would always just shut down and leave. Her mom thought that Maya wasn't impacted by what she said, so she took it to even more hurtful places each time they fought, looking for some kind of *reaction*, looking for confirmation that she *mattered* to Maya.

Though she went about seeking it in the wrong way, Maya's mom ultimately wanted connection. So many of us experienced childhoods in which our parents were self-centered and emotionally reactive. We mistook their reactivity for love in order to feel safe, in order to belong to our family. When you grow up in a household where chaos is the default, calm feels foreign and wrong. In adulthood, we lash out and create drama in order to receive the attention we now misinterpret as love. We seek a reaction because a reaction—any reaction—affirms that we are worthy of attention. It's part of the great unlearning that we must do as adults. Love doesn't ask you to perform and create drama to be worthy of it. Love is available. But of course, that is not what most of us learned as children. We instead learned that love was scarce.

When Maya was able to bring her mother inside her process, inside her feelings, thoughts, and reactions, the level of intimacy created immediately started to dissolve the walls each had built up around her heart. By modeling Conscious Communication, Maya invited her mother to take a deep dive into her mechanics, too, blessing both of them with a new perspective on and understanding of each other. What is so radical about this approach is that it asks the people communicating to consider each other's trauma. It encourages heart-led communication. It pushes you to make an effort to bring compassion and empathy back into the conversation for a holistic understanding of who is speaking, so true listening can take place. It allows for whole-person listening and whole-person understanding. We don't just hear words and look for how to win the argument, we listen to the whole person with love. Even when someone says something hurtful, Conscious Communication challenges you to take into account that hurt people hurt people.

The beauty of this work is that it not only evolves your relationships and pushes your communication to deeper levels of trust but also teaches you about your own patterns. When you have the courage to walk up to your friend and say, "Can I talk to you for a second?" and then tell them, "These are the things that come up for me when . . ." from a space of vulnerability and sacred connection, transformation happens. It's from this place that you actually get to learn about yourself and how to be a better friend. Every time you bring a pause into connection, every time you bring a deep breath into connection, you are setting in motion beneficial consequences that you cannot even begin to imagine are possible.

Conscious Communication is a skill set that can be used in moments when overwhelm or stress threaten to take over to help you bring your highest self to any conversation, argument, or disagreement. In these moments, we tend to lose our center and act and speak out of turn, which of course leads to harmful speech, guilt, anger, and resentment. These challenging emotions contract and restrict our view of reality. Instead of allowing challenging emotions to make our perspective polarized and partial, we have to use them as an opportunity for expansion.

We have an opportunity as we consciously communicate to choose our words wisely in order to cocreate a reality that benefits *everyone* involved. When we can take responsibility for what's happening inside us, we can come to the conversation without resorting to blame or projection. No more "You make me feel . . . !" A sacred friend takes full responsibility for their emotional state and the fact that no one can make us feel anything.

Think of it this way. Imagine a clear glass of water with a layer of sediment pooled at the very bottom. Someone else comes over and stirs the water, and it becomes muddy. You scream at them for "ruining" your glass of water, which is now undrinkable. But the impurities were there all along. It's the same with feelings. We might scream at someone, "Look at what you did to me! I feel this way because of you!" but the unmet needs were already there—we were just made aware of them. The sediment at the bottom of the water glass is like our karma, our shadow, our unmet needs, emotional baggage, unhealed hurts, and wounds. It's our conditioning. When we are in sacred friendship mode, we welcome the stirring.

The Reality of Grief

Grief? Yes, grief. Darling, I get it if even now, you're shrinking back from this book in your hands. Or maybe you're arguing with me, talking back to the page: "What the eff does grief have to do with conflict? Why the hell are we talking about grief in a chapter *I thought* was about conflict and communication?" Well, let me ask you something. How can we talk about staying in the fire without talking about the most intolerable feeling of all—our fear of death? How can we talk about coming to awareness of our own needs without talking about awareness of our own mortality? How can we talk about connecting, about nonviolence and consciousness, when—out of fear and discomfort—we fail to hold space for those who are grieving, adding pain to their pain? How can we talk about friendship when so many are lost because we don't know how to meet each other's grief, let alone our own?

Let's take it back to the beginning with conflict, namely, our desire to avoid it. Avoiding conflict is a way of avoiding a clash, a situation in which two people at odds are both seeking to meet their needs. Conflict can feel terrifying not just because of the intense emotions it arouses but also because of what seems to be at stake: the relationship itself. Our culture has trained us to believe that meeting one person's needs means forfeiting the other's. That in conflict, there is a person at fault and a person in the right. In conflict, we fear being found to be to blame. We fear being bad. We fear the loss of our goodness. We fear that how the other person sees us will change; we fear that we will lose their love. We fear that we will lose *them*.

The fear of loss is the undercurrent of all conflict. Avoiding conflict is rooted in our fear of loss, and grief is our response to loss. We fear grief because confronting it, accepting it, means confronting and accepting the reality of loss. Consider this: maybe, just maybe, conflict would be less scary if we were less afraid of grief?

Our avoidance—of conflict, of loss, of grief—is ultimately what creates our suffering. Maybe you've heard the expression "Pain is inevitable, suffering is not." A lot of people claim the Buddha said this, and it is a principle of Buddhism that while pain is inevitable, suffering is a choice. I bring this up in part because of what the Buddha *did* say about suffering: life consists of it. This *doesn't* mean that life is only suffering, or that it doesn't include pleasure and joy—not at all. It does mean that our lives, prior to liberation, are defined by suffering, because our lives are defined by our constant choice to resist reality—to resist impermanence and reject pain. Once you get that, it's clear how even pleasure and joy are related to suffering. We are always desperately attempting to grasp onto the people and things we love, that which brings us pleasure and joy. We grasp because we want to keep the people and things we love as they are, to hold onto them forever, which is simply not possible. We hold on tenaciously to what can't be held. Nothing stays the same forever. When we grasp, when we refuse to accept impermanence, suffering *is* inevitable.

The truth is that everything is impermanent. This moment right now, with all its beauty and its sadness, won't come again—but another, different moment will. Time is always unfurling itself, and its passage inevitably creates change. Change is the other face of loss. Often when we talk about grief, we talk about it only in relation to the loss of someone or something meaningful to us: a loved one, a marriage, a friendship, a job, a dream. With loss always comes change, however, and change creates its own kind of losses: the loss of the person we once were, the loss of how we once understood life, the loss of unquestioned beliefs or values, the loss of security, the loss of what we imagined our lives would look like or be. Losses like these can be so destabilizing that they make us question reality itself. But these types of losses, which we also grieve, also bring with them a moment of possibility: a new way of seeing ourselves, a new orientation toward life, a new way of being. Change contains within it the force of life itself.

The same is true of grief. If we allow ourselves to experience grief, if we let the pain in rather than resist it, we open ourselves to life. In grief, we are oriented toward what's meaningful to us. We grieve because we love. There is no pain in loss if what we lose doesn't matter to us. To come to terms with impermanence is to understand the value and limitations of our time and to be proactive about how we choose to spend it, and with whom. And truly? If we refuse to accept this? We will be in constant suffering. When we neglect our grief, when we refuse to welcome it, the pain we feel has no way to move through us. It becomes stored in us, an ever-present discomfort that keeps us tense and contracted, angry and deeply unhappy.

Grief is different from suffering, because when we grieve, we are acknowledging that who or what we love is gone—we are acknowledging love itself. And we are in contact with impermanence. When we allow ourselves to feel the pain of grief, we also allow ourselves to feel the force and power of our love. If you can recognize that grief is about what you love and miss, what you could lose, and let yourself miss and love it, appreciate it, then you're in a much more honest relationship with life. We can't stop loss from happening. We can't stop pain from happening. The people we love will die. How we meet that heartbreak is within our power. As grief experts David Kessler and Louise Hay wrote, "A broken heart is also an open heart."[5]

Grief is the condition of being human. Make friends with it. Embracing grief—accepting the impermanence of life—transforms heartbreak into heart opening, allowing us to see beauty in the midst of sadness. There is no real experience of presence that is not threaded with grief. When we're deeply present, we are aware of the fact that everything is always changing, always moving, completely impermanent. And it's also only when we're deeply present that we are in a state of alertness to the beauty of the world. Grief is a paradox.

The deepest of paradoxes, though, is that we can't truly embrace our own lives if we work strenuously to avoid thinking about our own mortality. Embracing grief—accepting impermanence—does not just mean accepting that *other* people will die. It means accepting that *you* will die. I know, my darling; for many of us, the fear attached to confronting this—the fear of the unknown, the fear of erasure of the self—is beyond intolerable. Unfortunately, the hard truth is that actively suppressing thoughts of our own death only increases our anxiety around the subject. Our culture does not support us here. Not only are most of us far removed from the experience of death, which has become largely medicalized and removed from the home, but we live in an era obsessed with the denial of aging. The pursuit of youth—or at least youthful appearance—is held up as an act of (faux) self-love. Talk about grasping.

But if we can learn to sit with our fear, can it become the lodestar that guides us to a better understanding of our deepest needs? *We want to live so badly, but why? What do we really care about? How do we then prioritize those things?* If we can learn to sit with our fear, can it become our teacher? You don't need to wait to lose someone or experience a devastating loss to learn the lessons grief has to offer us, especially its most fundamental one—we need each other. Accepting the inevitability of our own deaths first and foremost, working to diminish our own anxiety around the topic, is one of the most profound ways we can meet and hold the grief of others. People who are grieving need their pain to be affirmed, to be recognized—not swept under the rug with platitudes designed to relieve our own discomfort. When we are unafraid, we can hold space for their pain and grief. In holding space for their grief, we also hold space for their love. We affirm and recognize that their loved one matters. And so do they.

Practice: Maranasati Meditation, or Death Awareness

Thich Nhat Hanh wrote, "Thanks to impermanence, everything is possible. Life itself is possible. If a grain of corn is not impermanent, it can never be transformed into a stalk of corn. If the stalk were not impermanent, it could never provide us with the ear of corn we eat. If your daughter is not impermanent, she cannot grow up to become a woman. Then your grandchildren would never manifest. So instead of complaining about impermanence, we should say, 'Warm welcome and long live impermanence.' We should be happy. When we can see the miracle of impermanence, our sadness and suffering will pass."[6]

I thought of this passage when my teacher, the Venerable Tenzin Chogkyi, told me that in her encounters with people at end of life, one of the greatest commonalities was a sense of regret and their struggle to come to terms with it. People's greatest regrets were almost always that they hadn't spent more time with their children, their friends, their families. Or they regretted they hadn't pursued love and connection enough. Nobody ever said, "I regret that I didn't work longer hours at the office."

Maranasati is the Buddhist practice of "death awareness," a form of meditation meant to deepen our appreciation of impermanence and reduce the suffering of attachment. Or, you know, help prevent us from a deathbed realization—followed by deep regret—that we wasted our life pursuing fleeting gratification rather than enduring connection.

Death awareness comes in many forms, some heavier (and more morbid) than others. You can begin to practice it simply by attuning your attention to the endings we witness in everyday life: the golden-brown dried grass on rolling California hills at the end of another hot summer, the darkening carrot peels and molding berries decomposing in your compost bin, the slim bleached bone of some unknown tiny animal you discovered on your last hike. Moments like these are organic memento mori, signaling the universal impermanence of all life.

A more classic—and slightly more advanced—maranasati meditation is reflecting on "The Nine Contemplations of Death" by the great eleventh-century Buddhist scholar and teacher Atiśa. The first three contemplations focus on the inevitability of death; the second three on the uncertainty of when it will arrive; and the final three on the fact that nothing can save you when it does come. I know, it's heavy stuff, but the idea is to really *know* in your bones, in your blood, in your marrow the preciousness of life and to understand that it is made precious by death.

Read the contemplations as many times as you'd like. Then, taking a comfortable seat, close your eyes, take a few deep breaths to invite relaxation into your body and mind, and reflect on them, allowing your feelings and thoughts to arise without judgment.

The Nine Contemplations of Death

1. Death is inevitable; all of us will die sooner or later.

2. Our life span is continuously decreasing.

3. Death will come whether or not you are prepared for it.

4. None of us know how long we will live; death can come at any time.

5. Death comes by many causes.

6. The human body is fragile.

7. When death arrives, our belongings are of no use to us.

8. Our loved ones cannot keep us from death.

9. Your body cannot help you at the time of death.

Chapter 6

Hiding in Plain Sight

While I was in India, practicing at my first retreat, I met an incredible Canadian Buddhist nun, Venerable Joan Nicell, with whom I'm still in touch today. She addressed the crowd with the warmest compassion on her face, kindness and love spilling from her eyes. I felt both so vividly, it was as if she reached through the crowd and held my face in her warm, gentle hands as she said, "You are not broken. There is nothing wrong with you. We are all innately good. We all have basic goodness inside us."

Listening to her speak, I straight up cried. Her words struck me like lightning. At the time, the concept of our innate goodness was *really* far out for me and took me for such a ride. For as long as I could remember, I had felt like there was something inherently wrong with me. I had spent so much of my life feeling deficient, innately bad, like I was irreparably broken because of my queerness. I felt like I deserved everything terrible that had happened to me and that I didn't deserve anything better moving forward.

The mistakes I had made and the harm I had caused others were both the evidence and the confirmation that I was deeply flawed. This sense that I was fundamentally damaged had kept me from making authentic connections—how could I ever allow anyone to see my "real" self?—and also shackled me to my suffering. Those feelings that drove me to hide, that compelled me to numb my pain with drugs and alcohol? They all came down to the same thing: shame.

Shame is one of the most basic human emotions there is, but also one of the most complex and damaging. It is literally a *self-conscious* emotion, a perception of ourselves as inadequate and unworthy of love, of belonging, of acceptance. I consider shame to be one of our most basic emotions not only because it's almost universally experienced but also because it's a foundational emotion, one of the basic building blocks of self-awareness, stemming from a fundamental mistake in perception. We got the instructions wrong, we misread the blueprints: the part that says that at the core of our being, we're essentially good? Yeah, most of us skipped right over that. And when we don't know we're fundamentally good, we mistake our deepest selves, our hearts, our essence, our being. We believe, instead, that we're fundamentally *not good*, that we are, in other words, bad. That the bad things that happen to us and the bad things we do are not actions but *identity*: confirmation of who we know we are, deep down. It's the ultimate confirmation bias.

Over and over again, my experiences as a teacher, as a student—as simply a person in the world, trying my best but sometimes fumbling, just like everyone else—have shown me that the core wound for most people is this fundamental sense of shame. It might be subtle, but eventually, as you listen to people's stories, to their pain, to their dramas, you'll find that tying everything together is the thread of shame, though they may not have access to it or even be aware of it. Underneath all our problems is that very subtle thread. Because when we don't think we're good? Then we punish ourselves, and the way we punish ourselves is by people pleasing, by overworking, by staying in our stories for too long, by creating self-fulfilling prophecies, addictions, and suffering—chasing that confirmation. The even more perverse part? These punishments are also a form of relief. They make it possible to hide from ourselves and others, so we never have to risk really coming into contact with that shame.

When we exist in an ongoing state of shame, there's no hope for sacred friendship. The love and compassion we offer others are hollow because we still believe that people can be innately bad. No matter how much effort we make to unlearn the poisonous behaviors around how we relate to others, no matter how long we stay in the fire, no matter our seeming acceptance of impermanence, ultimately we can't authentically and deeply connect with others if the connection to ourselves isn't there. Shame is the greatest obstacle to connection.

The only way to loosen shame's grip on us is to rob it of its power, to make it less threatening. To do that, we have to dismantle it, to recognize it as a misapprehension of reality. That starts by understanding how shame breeds and the harms it creates as it causes us to hide from others, but also ourselves. When we understand how shame functions in relationship, it becomes clear that some of our strategies for connection are actually mechanisms for coping with shame. Knowing this, we can start embracing vulnerability as the antidote for shame, as long as we hold fast to the distinction between trauma dumping and being intentionally vulnerable. Practicing vulnerability leads to acceptance, which creates space for transfiguration—the transformation and sanctification of meaning that, finally, not only grants us permission to stop chasing confirmation of our brokenness but also allows wisdom and miracles to emerge.

Hiding in Plain Sight

The fundamental shame generated by our separation from our goodness is always there, thrumming along in the background. Sometimes it emerges, though, with more or less force (and more or less self-awareness) in daily life, triggered by internal thoughts and judgments after we fail to meet our own expectations, standards, or ideas about who we're supposed to be. Of course, these ideas don't just appear out of nowhere; they are internalized messages about what it means to be acceptable, to be lovable, to be worthy of belonging. We receive these messages from our upbringing and environment—though rarely, if ever, is the message "You are worthy just as you are," because these messages are, of course, rooted in the same misunderstanding of our basic nature.

From our earliest moments, our family and our culture transmit these dispatches to us. We begin absorbing messages about what it means to be a person worthy of love and belonging without even realizing it. Some of it we learn explicitly: from the expressed values of our families, from the rules and expectations of social codes and norms, from the ideology and morality of religion, from the economic systems in which we're caught (I think it's worth stressing here that a society like ours, which treats people as transactional commodities, actively breeds shame). And some of it we learn from modeling—not by what institutions or people profess or say but by what they practice, what they do, including *when* they *withhold* love or belonging.

If we grow up with parents whose love is conditional, who don't accept us the way we are, we internalize the message that we are not adequate the way we are and that the only path to love is to meet certain conditions. Maybe that means repressing certain feelings, hopes, or dreams. Maybe it means being an athlete, a straight-A student, a competitive musician. Maybe it means following a certain career path. These internalized messages become the lens through which we view the world. Parental shame is also contagious: if we grow up with parents who experience a lot of shame—shame about their financial status, shame about being immigrants, shame about their appearance, shame about family secrets, any of a million things—we also learn to be ashamed of those aspects of ourselves or the potential for them. Our old friend trauma is the GOAT when it comes to shame. If we grow up in emotionally or physically abusive homes, it's especially easy to internalize a belief that there is something wrong with *us*. For a child, whose parents—however shitty—are the center of their world and the locus of their love, what other reason could there be for the pain they inflict? Why would these all-knowing, godlike beings hurt us unless we deserved it? And while trauma often starts at home, the world at large doles it out unhesitatingly to those of us who "fail" to comply with its norms, those of us outside the structures of power, be we poor, queer, trans, Black, Brown, female, femme, the wrong religion, the wrong ethnicity—other.

Early on, when we first experience withholding, rejection, or trauma, "Shame Logic" teaches us "Something bad happened to me, so I must be bad." Shame Logic teaches us that there is no distinction between the self and the actions perpetrated on it or experienced by it. Though this line of reasoning is incredibly painful, it at least makes sense of that which has no sense. It can be more confusing and even painful for our minds to try to process that something bad happened to us "for no reason," because we mistake "reason" for "meaning." Something that has "no reason" is arbitrary. Something that is arbitrary is random. But our pain doesn't feel arbitrary or random; it feels deeply personal. The idea that we experience pain in service to "nothing" is unbearable. On top of that, the stigma (i.e., external shame) around certain kinds of trauma can also make us feel tainted, "ruined," or permanently broken: something bad happened to me, and now I am bad. In this way and so many others, shame is also an aspect of conditioning.

No matter where our shame lives, it feels critical, desperately important, to conceal it from other people. Not just the "source" of the shame (remember, the ultimate source is a mistake in perception) but the shame itself—after all, Shame Logic 101 tells us that only a bad person would have something to be ashamed about. As Dr. Wurzman described it to me, "Shame is one of the most potent types of social pain there is." It also serves a dual purpose as a signal of the threat of social disconnection: "It is an actual physiological reflex to the threat of rejection, of being out of connection with a group," explained Dr. Wurzman.[1]

In a way, then, shame can be a useful emotion. The potential of experiencing shame is a pretty effective deterrent to enforcing certain meaningful social norms, ethics, and morals, you know? Yeah, we should uphold all those prosocial dictates—don't hurt others, don't lie, etc.—*because we believe in them*, but we're all only human. We will make mistakes and act in ways that don't always accord with our shared values. So, yes, it's not a bad thing per se to be aware of the fact that if you transgress a meaningful norm, that if you do something opposed to our agreed-upon ideas of what's right and wrong, you might feel like shit about yourself as a person. Remembering that, and choosing not to behave that way because you don't want to feel like that, is not a negative. We *should* be in touch with what we believe and strive to live accordingly. Reminding ourselves that we will feel bad about ourselves if we don't is, frankly, positive.

Shame is also different from guilt. When we experience guilt, we experience awareness of wrongdoing. It's "I did something bad," not "I am bad." Shame is the awareness of the *self* as wrong or bad, a failure to separate the self from our actions. It's "I am bad" as opposed to "I did something bad." Shame directs our focus inward, where guilt directs us to focus on the feelings of others—an understanding that our behavior has caused harm. Both shame and guilt can function like our own built-in alarm systems, alerting us that we're not living in integrity with our values, that we're risking our belonging.

And we *should* value healthy belonging (or I wouldn't be writing this book)—none of us wants to be kicked out of the tribe. And look, if you do experience shame or guilt following a harmful behavior, and that sense of shame prevents you from behaving that way again or the guilt pushes you to take accountability and repair the damage, then . . . I don't think those are emotions we should necessarily identify as bad. That kind of shame—shame that is time bound (i.e., it comes and then it goes; it's fleeting), that involves recognition of our values, and that exists in sync with our desire to create beneficial karma rather than perpetuate negative karma—is what I call "acute shame." Acute shame, though possibly more intense than other difficult or uncomfortable feelings, is still one we can learn to sit with. We can process it in the body, remembering that it is a feeling and that feelings are transient—not life sentences.

That's not the kind of shame I was carrying with me when I broke down that morning in India. And that's not the kind of shame we're talking about here, the shame burdening so many of us, preventing us from living as our full selves, preventing us from really *living*. The sense that something is fundamentally wrong with you? That you are inadequate, broken, bad, damaged, flawed, irredeemable, unworthy of love or belonging? That you're not and never will be good enough? That's *fundamental shame*, shame that has calcified and become your identity. In usurping your identity, fundamental shame erodes your sense of self, your ability to know yourself: its very premise is the denial of innate goodness.

On the scale of uncomfortable feelings, fundamental shame is unique, and that's what makes it so sneaky and dangerous. It's not just uncomfortable; it is intolerable because it involves our very conception of self. Fundamental shame is not transient, because it has become our state of being, and we can't afford to come into full contact with it. The threat to our ego is too great. After all, if we allow ourselves to really touch the unworthiness we believe is the core of who we are, why would we carry on? Shame is a judgment of who we are, and we avoid it in order to survive. This doesn't mean that this kind of shame has to be a life sentence. It means that if we want to be free of it, we need to find a way to touch it. We need to learn we don't need to fear it.

But because contact with it is so threatening, we are unwilling to sit with fundamental shame, to allow ourselves to feel it, so it doesn't move through us, up and out. The problem is that if our darkness doesn't come up and out, we can't see it, and if we can't see it, we can't integrate it. So it lurks within us, festering. It's always there, whispering in the background. It's a saboteur, deliberately destroying and obstructing our dreams behind the scenes. Shame operates in silence and secrecy, so much so that most people don't even know what they're ashamed of, they've spent so long looking away. Whatever it is, though—we have to hide it from others.

So the irony becomes that shame—already painful in and of itself—often produces loneliness because it causes us to isolate ourselves as a protective mechanism against rejection. As Dr. Wurzman laid it out, the loneliness produced by shame then causes "a double whammy of pain—not only are you alone, which causes pain, you feel shame for being alone." And the vicious cycle becomes more intractable. We run away, we hide, we isolate. And as we learned way back at the beginning of this book, isolation and loneliness are killing us. The isolation and loneliness don't have to be literal—and, I'd argue, often are not. Plenty of people I know—maybe even you, there on the other side of this page—are hiding in plain sight, surrounded by friends, leading an enviable life, working so fucking hard all the while to isolate the part of themselves that feels shame. To hide it, to keep it pushed down, pushed away, locked up in the dark. Never willingly outing that part of themselves to others.

But when you walk through life feeling, deep down, that you're an innately a bad person, you always feel like you have a secret to hide. You're always looking not just over your shoulder but in your mirror, hoping that no one is going to find out. It's the ultimate impostor syndrome. And you know what? That "I'm perfectly okay" mask you're wearing? It's not doing as fantastic a job as you think it is. The workaholism, the perpetual busyness and distraction? The self-medication? I see it, and I know you do, too. We all use these behaviors to conceal our shame, not only from others but first and foremost from ourselves.

A person who buries themself in work relies on it as their main source of value—they've lost touch with their innate goodness (or never known it) and use work to distract themself from the uncomfortable feeling in the body begging for their attention. That uncomfortable feeling? It's shame asking you to receive its true message: not that you are unworthy but that you urgently need to rediscover your innate goodness. The same goes for someone who glorifies being busy all the time as if busyness were God. That's because in moments of quiet, of silence, it's much harder to avoid the shame trapped in your body. The numbing agent of distraction has been removed. Shame lurks in the scrolling through social media, in the myriad ways we distract ourselves from the quiet. Shame, like any feeling, lives in the body, but we tend to pay attention to it only when it becomes an emergency. The "maintenance" signal on the dashboard has been illuminated for months, but now the car has caught on fire on the highway. Don't let this be you if you can help it. Trust me, fires are expensive, honey. Shame, untended, can destroy you. That's the real irony. You don't actually have anything to fear if you face it head-on, even though it feels like you have everything to lose. The key is learning to recognize it, to understand how it's hiding, to drop your mask, and to sanctify it.

Belong to Yourself

One of the more typical relational responses to shame that I encounter is people pleasing. Nobody wants to think of themself as a "people pleaser." It just sounds . . . icky. When you think of a people pleaser, what is called to mind? Someone who can't say no. Someone who is always putting the needs of others before their own. Someone who doesn't have an identity outside how they help make life nicer for the people around them. Someone who has subsumed their own needs and wants and may no longer even know what they are. Surely, this could never be me! And yet . . . maybe it is. People pleasing isn't about being "weak" or "strong." It's about strategically diverting the gaze of others away from yourself. It's about manipulating perception to shield yourself. It's about selling yourself a particular story so you don't have to take accountability for yourself. And a lot of us do it—it's one of the most common relational shame responses I encounter, especially among people who already have a healthy, natural tendency to care for others.

Let's clear that up right away: finding joy in making others happy, in creating a beautiful life for the people around you, in caring for others, in enjoying acceptance and belonging, in being people-oriented, in seeking harmony is not people pleasing. The desire to please, to create pleasure or beauty, to care, to soothe, to make peace is not, in and of itself, a shadow trait. If it were, we'd have a serious problem. Our teachers, our artists, our caregivers, our therapists, our counselors, our diplomats, our saints (and our sinners) . . . our lives would be unimaginable without them. The nuance is that the motivation behind the behavior is not transactional (obviously, I don't mean that teachers and caregivers shouldn't be paid for their labor—in fact, these should probably be the highest-paid careers in a just world): the person who engages in "pleasing" or caring for others isn't doing it to get something back from the person they are pleasing—the motivation is their own pleasure. In other words, the intention is heart opening, not heart closing.

When I talk about people pleasing as a shame response, I'm talking about constantly and compulsively engaging in behaviors that secure others' view of us as helpful, good, trustworthy, and kind, regardless of the toll it takes on us, the bandwidth we have to do so, or how we really feel. Okay, maybe it seems like this behavior is pretty harmless, not counting the harm it does to the people pleaser. At least they're putting good out in the world, right? Honestly, no. This kind of behavior is a form of manipulation, and it's especially insidious precisely because it's not obviously harmful. Its first function is to assuage our own feelings of inadequacy and unworthiness produced by shame, yes. But its second function is preventing others from knowing how we really feel, from knowing what's actually going on under the layers. Most people pleasers are unconsciously manipulative and unwilling to let others into their inner world.

People pleasers view life through a transactional, capitalistic lens, always unconsciously needing something in return. Everything that they do for others has to have an outcome that works to mask or silence their shame. This is clear when people pleasing becomes a case of martyr syndrome, as it often does. The interesting thing about martyr syndrome is that it also has a double function. The obvious one is garnering sympathy (again, a way to seek external validation in order to silence shame), but the less obvious one is avoiding having to care for yourself, avoiding having to do any work on yourself, avoiding making peace with your past, all of which allow you not only to avoid your shame but also to remain unaccountable for yourself. You're unwilling to take care of yourself, so you take care of others. But remember, honey, taking care of all beings means taking care of *all* beings: it starts with you. There is a false element to the care a people pleaser provides because the ultimate goal is to abdicate personal responsibility for the quality of your own life—*How can you expect me to meditate . . . go to therapy . . . exercise . . . eat better when I'm so busy caring for everyone else?* People pleasing makes it easier to stay in a victim mindset and perpetuate a cycle of blame.

At its core, people pleasing slowly erodes our sense of self even further. Shame isolates us from authentic connection with ourselves, and people pleasing—as a way to keep shame at bay—just keeps eating away at our foundation. The more you prioritize pleasing others, the more you deprioritize your own needs. The longer you do this, the harder it becomes to even know what your needs are. Conflict becomes unbearable, and standing by your values (if you even have true clarity on what they're comprised of) becomes harder and harder. Because people pleasers lose hold of who they are, they tend to be chronically unsatisfied. They wish they were hanging out with someone else, they wish there was different music playing, they wish they had ordered tacos once the burrito arrives (I'm with them). It doesn't matter if they're sitting in the most beautiful garden under the bluest sky. They're not content in the here and now. They're tripping about a past that was better than the present. They are, mentally, anywhere but here. They believe that happiness is contingent—if I do X . . . when Y happens . . . then I'll be happy.

Why does this happen? Because when you don't know who you are, you don't know what you want. When you don't know what you want, you're not satisfied with what you have. And you tend to focus on the wants of others. It's a vicious circle. Not only that, but you *can't* meet the needs of the present moment. People pleasers aren't wrong that something is missing, but it's not what they think it is. It's an awareness of and connection to our essential goodness that enables us to be with uncomfortable feelings, that allows us to stay present. It's meeting the moment and, in the resulting pause, learning the next best action. You can only know the next best action when you've brought in a moment of pause. Chronically dissatisfied people never pause.

When you never pause, it becomes easier to tamp down those feelings of shame because there's no time to reflect on how you're feeling or why (let alone feel those feelings). It becomes easier to ignore the inner voice. And this makes it easier than ever to people please. This also makes it easier to commit small harms against ourselves that have large impact: you might be a vegetarian but eat meat to make other people feel at ease. You might have a drink to fit in even though you know that it is not the best decision for you. These small actions leave an imprint in the mind and encourage even greater actions that are out of alignment with our convictions, our integrity, and true connection.

People pleasing is a mostly one-to-one behavior that takes place in individual relationships. We may even be people pleasers with one person but not another—depending on how much their acceptance means to us or how much we feel is at stake. In the context of a group, people pleasing becomes a drive to "fit in." All the small ways in which we've compromised our integrity through people pleasing, all the times we failed to listen to and honor ourselves, set us up beautifully to seek belonging at this larger level regardless of what it may cost us. Group acceptance is a powerful drug, and many of us are chasing the high, whether online or in person. A desire to be accepted, to belong, to be loved is healthy and natural, of course. These are not shame responses in and of themselves—of course not. The confusion happens when, in service to stifling our shame, we ignore ourselves in the process and focus our energy on external ways to find this sense of belonging we seek.

Maybe you've found acceptance in a group you don't even like, but you continue to spend time in it rather than be alone. Membership satisfies the hurting part of you that wants to fill the lonely void as quickly as possible. Maybe, at a surface level, you obtain the belonging you seek, but you feel totally out of place. You're sitting there mentally judging and criticizing the people you're choosing to surround yourself with. This is not freedom. On a neurochemical level, yes, you are experiencing a degree of community, but ask yourself, what does it cost you to have a seat at this table? If it costs you your integrity, this is a good sign that this acceptance is misplaced and this particular group is not for you.

It might sound juvenile, but the desire to "fit in" (and trust me, even misfits want to be recognized as such by other iconoclasts) doesn't just go away when you leave junior high. A lot of us have lived long enough that, just from life experience, we've been places and behaved in ways that weren't in integrity with who we were, because we wanted to belong, especially when we were young. We know what that feels like when we look back. That doesn't disappear in adulthood, though—it just becomes harder to recognize. Because we live in delusion, because we're so afraid to feel our feelings, because of our conditioning and lack of freedom, we might not be aware that we're choosing to be in a group of friends or in community with a group of people that *we don't actually like*—or, worse, that are costing us our integrity.

So ask yourself, "Is sitting at this table costing me something?" Ask yourself, "Is this group dynamic, are these people, are their values in integrity with what I believe?" Answering those questions can be surprisingly hard and uncomfortable, so I often like to reframe them for myself as "Am I inspired when I leave?" What does it mean to be inspired by another person or people? I don't mean you hop off FaceTime and paint the next *Mona Lisa*. When I ask myself, "Do I feel inspired?" I'm checking to see whether my interaction has left me relaxed enough to have a new perspective on life, even if that shift is tiny, even if it's just a little something. Our friends, sacred friends in particular, are meant to help share the burden, help carry the heaviness of life. When you're hanging out with a group of three or four people, for those hours together, you're not shouldering life by yourself. And because of that, you arrive at a state relaxed enough that your nervous system calms, you're not on high alert, your view widens: there is a capacity to see your life, the little things, with a little more grace and generosity, a slightly different perspective. One of my close creative partners always leaves me renewed after we get through a working session, even when it's long or I'm being pushed to stretch myself intellectually or emotionally—I hang up and feel that "I can do this." I'm energized and excited about the work, even if it's hard. That's what we want from a friend—that's inspiration.

We desperately want to belong, but first we have to belong to ourselves. One of the ways we can lessen belonging seeking that is shame based is by remembering that approval does not equal belonging. Belonging is not necessarily about being "liked." Belonging is about a shared kinship, a shared value system. It includes an acceptance of our full selves by others and a sense that we are safe with others. Being liked is a nice benefit of belonging, but it shouldn't be the first thing you're seeking. Approval is misleading when you're not already in tune with what you value in yourself and others. So often, when we seek acceptance and approval, we don't even consider whether or not *we* like the people in question, whether or not *we* find them energizing and inspiring.

Years ago, one of my friends, Joey, was struggling with the fact that his neighbor hadn't invited him over for the frequent after-work drinks they held on their patio. Joey was new to the apartment complex, whereas several people in the building had known each other for the previous five years or so—this was the cocktail group. We were out for brunch with our other friend, Sarah, as Joey told the story. "I don't think they like me very much," Joey told us, "and I don't know why.

But it really sucks to be excluded." I'll never forget Sarah's response to Joey. "Maybe they don't like you," Sarah said matter-of-factly. I was kind of shocked at her blasé attitude—she wasn't trying to convince Joey that he had misunderstood or that his new neighbors must of course like him, because how could they not?

Joey looked confused and slightly offended. "I hope not?" he said in a questioning tone.

Sarah looked at him levelly as I sat there trying to process the interaction. "Why? Does everybody have to like you?" she said.

"No . . . I guess not," Joey said. He sounded doubtful.

"Joey," Sarah continued, "have you even asked yourself if you like them?"

I looked at Joey, and he looked at me. He paused before answering. "No," he admitted.

"Okay, well, think about it for a minute. Do you like them?" Sarah sounded a little impatient. Honestly, this was a revelation for me as much as it was for Joey. I was eager to hear how he would answer.

"Not really," Joey said. We all sat there in silence for a moment. "Actually, every time I do go over there, I'm always waiting to leave," he confessed. Joey had been so focused on wanting to belong and be accepted that he hadn't paid attention to or even tried to identify how he felt in that context or community. For the people pleaser in me, hearing Sarah's implied point that not everyone has to like you—as simple as it was—was a necessary reminder. Even though I've dealt with the feeling of not being liked by everyone for as long as I can remember, even I forget: not everyone has to like you. It's not a crisis or emergency if you're not for everyone.

This was life-altering because it was one of the first times I grasped that it doesn't mean I'm doing something wrong or that there must be something wrong with me if another person doesn't like me. Not everyone is for everyone. Part of belonging to yourself and defeating Shame Logic is holding on to this simple truth. Ninety-nine percent of the time, whether or not someone likes you isn't even about you. It's not personal. The way others see us is mostly about them. Their karma leads to their perception of the world and the people in it.

I made so many mistakes because I wanted to belong, to be accepted, to fit in, to be liked. Until my late teens, I pretended to be straight. I wanted to fit into the heteronormative narrative. I didn't want to be left out. I caused myself tremendous harm, and I harmed other people because of this need. Even after I first came out, I tried to be "acceptably" queer: more straight-passing in my presentation, less femme, less flamboyant—I didn't allow myself to be uninhibited in my self-expression because part of me was still ashamed of being gay. I was out, but I was still preoccupied with acceptance by society at large. I still had all these shoulds and should nots dictating my appearance, even though these rules were premised on a culture that was homophobic. Even in my own queer community at that time, there was a hierarchy of beauty and sexual desirability modeled on conventional ideas of masculinity. I pushed back against my innate desire to try to be "one of the boys." But you know what? It wasn't until I started showing up in my full glory that my content went viral. Once I decided, "I like seeing myself as art," and started living by that, that was when my audience quadrupled in size. Once I started belonging to myself, I started finding belonging with others—and offering it, authentically—in ways I couldn't have imagined before.

Being at peace with yourself is one of the most profound ways to find belonging with yourself. What does it mean to be at peace? Peace is the acceptance of what is. Being at peace is a choice we make. The nature of this choice is embodied in this wisdom that my teacher, the Venerable Sarah Thresher, once shared with me: Whatever comes, let it come. Whatever goes, let it go. Have no need for anything.

When I feel anxious or disconnected, or a wave of tension kicks in and I start to apply stories to those feelings, I am not at peace. But if I feel a wave of anxiety, disconnection, or tension coming and I don't storify, I just allow myself to notice it—"Oh, wow, I'm feeling disconnected; I'm feeling tense"—and let it wash over me. If I'm able to name it and accept it, then I am at peace. Being at peace is accepting that what you feel is only one moment in time and meeting that moment. Maybe it's a long moment; maybe it's many moments, an hour, two hours, a whole day, sure. But you meet it: you don't storify it, you don't concretize it by making it the definition of your day, you don't solidify it as an aspect of your personality; you allow your awareness to touch it, to make contact with that wisdom *Whatever comes, let it come. Whatever goes, let it go. Have no need for anything.* "Okay, this is coming up for me. I allow it to come up. And this is leaving. I allow it to leave. I don't need anything." That last piece is maybe the most important in understanding acceptance: to not need anything is our reminder that we don't have to "fix" anything before accepting. Acceptance doesn't require anything; it isn't contingent on doing something. Peace is the acceptance of what is. When we accept what is, we're not resisting reality or struggling against it. We accept that life is constantly changing—impermanence. We stop grasping, though we are desperate to hold on, because we understand that there is nothing to hold on to. Whatever comes, let it come. Whatever goes, let it go.

Acceptance is the first step in belonging to yourself. Only then can you start to experience true belonging in a way that will illuminate you so that when you enter a room, people will immediately be drawn to you. We're all drawn to people who exude peace, and peace cannot be performative. Peace is nonverbal, energetic; it's a fragrance in the air. It's in the way a person carries themself through the world. It's why I was so drawn to the Buddhist nuns I met at the beginning of my journey: because they have unwavering access to peace. It is a choice they keep making. Being at peace isn't about going around greeting everyone with "Namaste. Love and light." How many times have you sat in front of a meditation teacher or anyone in the wellness space and they're *performing* peace? It's something you can see through. You ended up being drawn to this book, to me, even though I am wild, loud, bold, queer, sassy, because I'm not performing peace. I'm experiencing peace. Not all the time, no, but I can say that I know peace. Not "know" as in something that I memorized after studying, but as a gnosis *I know in my heart.*

Being at peace encourages true belonging. It encourages healthy behavior and boundaries. Those who desperately want to belong are easily influenced by others. But when you're at peace, there is nothing desperate about you. When you feel a glimpse of peace around a person or in a place, follow that feeling, learn to recognize it so you can learn the difference between performance and experience. When you are at peace, you can fully take in and consider the opinions of others because you trust yourself. You belong to yourself.

Acceptance of what is, being at peace, makes it easier to overcome resistance to being vulnerable. When we are at peace, we can more readily risk vulnerability because we know that whatever the response to that vulnerability, we still belong to ourselves. No one can take that away. When we're vulnerable, we destigmatize the painful parts of the human experience. When we're vulnerable, we deprive shame of what it needs to thrive: darkness. In light, shame withers.

Trauma Dumping

As an emotion, shame is a twin to fear. We conceal our shame—we people please, we risk our integrity in order to belong—because we're afraid of being exposed. We fear that if people knew our "real" selves (i.e., the selves we imagine to be fundamentally flawed and broken), we'd be rejected. We fear the pain of rejection, and we fear being alone, so we engage in behaviors that are, ironically, antithetical to real connection. In reality, a willingness to be vulnerable, to be the kind of person who is, as Brené Brown puts it, "willing to demonstrate what it looks like to risk and endure failure, disappointment and regret . . . willing to feel their own hurt instead of working it out on other people . . . willing to own their stories, live their values, and keep showing up"[2] is what fosters meaningful connection.

When we encounter people who are honest about the trajectory of their life—the inescapable fact that it is always, for everyone, a mix of attempts and victories, of losses and successes, of pain and joy—how they feel about it, and what they've learned, we trust them, because we know the texture of truth. Most of us can sniff out a bullshit artist if we're really paying attention. When we encounter someone who focuses on growth rather than achievement, who isn't ashamed of where they've been, we feel less shame ourselves—we feel invited to see our own stories as open-ended, still being written, rather than a collection of narratives with unhappy endings or fixed meanings.

Being vulnerable means sacrificing your ego, your comfort, to allow others—but especially yourself—to see the parts of yourself that might elicit judgment: not just the events of your life but your hopes and dreams, your fears, so that you can truly know and be known. It means being honest about your feelings, not just what has happened to you or what you've done. But being vulnerable with others in that inspiring, energizing, and deeply authentic way is trickier than it seems, because many of us misunderstand what it means to be vulnerable in the first place. Too many of us mistake oversharing, often uninvited, for vulnerability—in other words, "trauma dumping."

Trauma dumping is a form of disempowered vulnerability. When we trauma dump, we're rarely connecting—instead of engaging in a give-and-take, we're usually absorbed in a monologue that is hyperfocused on cataloging our pain, suffering, and trauma. Yes, of course people can connect through discovering they've endured similar pain. There is relief in knowing that someone else out there gets it, that you're not alone, that others have been where you've been or where you are. But when we're trauma dumping, our intention is rarely actually connection—even if we think it is. Instead, it's positioning ourselves as a victim and seeking pity while laying blame. In a way, it's eerily similar to the intention behind people pleasing—it's validation seeking. We think we're looking for connection, but what we're looking for is a response. Connection is a mutual state of being, not a response.

I call trauma bonding "disempowered vulnerability" because it's a form of looping into destructive behaviors and thought patterns. When you are not empowered by what has happened or is happening in your life, you end up replaying the same horror movie in your mind 250,070,500 times in hopes of finding another outcome. You believe that by telling the story over and over and over and over and over again, something else will happen. You're putting a period instead of a comma on the statement of your life. You're allowing the hurts and the pains and the tragic parts of your story to define you, to be *the* story rather than a part of the story.

How do you know if you're engaging in trauma dumping or disempowered vulnerability in general? Do you find yourself engaging, internally, in a trauma competition—judging whether or not someone else has had it "as hard" as you? Do you find yourself thinking, "My traumas are more difficult than yours" or "My pain is greater than yours"? Take a hard look at the intentions behind your sharing. What are you seeking when you share? And when are you sharing? Are you always responding to others' experiences with a story about yourself? Have you been invited to share? In other words, is it welcome? How close are you with the person with whom you're sharing? This last one is critical. Intimacy is something that, ideally, we build through trust. In a way, telling people you don't know well intensely private stories can actually make them trust you less—it's confusing to be on the receiving end of an emotionally charged conversation with a person you don't feel close to. It can create a feeling of obligation rather than closeness. It may also diminish the nature of what you've shared for the person listening—after all, if this were so significant to you, why would you be telling them?

It's interesting to me how trauma has become a form of currency on social media, which relies on very quickly generating a (false) sense of familiarity and rapport between audience and subject—parasocial relationships, baby. There are a lot of people I respect out there on the 'Gram whose entire online persona is their trauma. Their bios—"survivor of this," "living with this," etc.—are nothing more than their diagnosis. Look, I understand deeply that certain phrases are a quick way to signal shared experience to people who might be looking for community, insight, or resources. And that is awesome, without question. But for me, if that's the only point of connection you're trying to make as a "leader" in whatever area, if it's all-encompassing, then there's a degree of disempowered vulnerability at work, and a perpetuation of that as a desirable way to relate to people. We need people who are honest about what they are living with, but why not write "Advocate for CPTSD" rather than "Living with CPTSD"? Make it about the work you do, the compassion, rather than about yourself.

There is nothing to be ashamed of or embarrassed about, of course, but centering yourself, and centering yourself as this one thing—your trauma—is not how intimacy and connection work. The moment we're in glorifies and celebrates the experience of trauma as a badge of honor, as a marker of moral superiority, but that's a losing game. It's an ego game, no different, really, from the people touting their religious convictions as a sign of their supposed enlightenment.

How long have you been replaying that story and using it as your gateway to connection? How long have you allowed that period in your life to be the definition of your story? The hardest thing about being in this state is that it's so hard to know when enough is enough. Obviously, we want to be able to talk about the fires we've walked through. As we grow close with people, we want them to understand the forces that have shaped us. So where is the line drawn? The simplest way to think about it is this: we're in a state of disempowered vulnerability when we haven't yet arrived at the place where wisdom is. You've pathologized rather than integrated whatever it is that you're sharing. Engaging with the story hasn't helped shape a new perspective for you.

Life is your best detective here. Are the people around you in the same state? Do you find yourself attracted to other people who constantly rehash their trauma? Sometimes the state of disempowered vulnerability can be subtle. Maybe it's the type of TV you're watching, the food you're eating, the drugs or alcohol you're consuming, or the music you're listening to that contributes to your state. These behaviors become unconscious, making them even harder to identify. As you know, misery loves company. Look from the outside in, and let your relationships and the people in your life show you if you are in a well-intentioned misery loop and avoiding true connection. As we know, whatever we put our attention on grows. Do you want to put your attention on suffering or illumination? While engaging in disempowered vulnerability may feel good in the short term, you're actually sowing more misery seeds in the garden of your mind and causing more harm than good.

Intentional Vulnerability

Buddhism teaches us that intention is everything—the single most impactful action we can take to repair or prevent harmful behaviors is to correct the intention, our motivation, behind our actions and address them at the root. Keeping this in mind, we can begin to unlearn the habits of disempowered vulnerability by focusing on being *intentionally* vulnerable: keeping our intentions at the front of our mind when we share emotionally intimate thoughts, feelings, or experiences, such as anything about which we feel shame. The most direct way to be clear about your intentions is so simple that it's almost annoying. Ask yourself, before you speak, "Am I doing this to benefit others? Or am I doing this only to benefit myself?" The idea is to be constantly aware of your objective, to know your "why." Once you know the answer, you're guided by liberation-affirming choices. Instead of "I want to share the mistakes I made with others so they can tell me it's not that bad," your reasoning is "I want to share the mistakes I made with others so they don't make the same mistakes I did and don't have to experience the same suffering." Finding out that, yeah, your mistakes really weren't that bad is a happy bonus, a lovely moment of connection and new awareness gained, rather than an ego-driven motivation.

Intentional vulnerability reminds you to speak about your pain in order to inspire people rather than provoke their pity. When you speak from a place of intentional, authentic vulnerability, you invite people to illuminate the intention of their hearts, the benevolence that lives within them. Intentional, authentic vulnerability helps establish true connection, making you a safe place for others to land. Remember, shame isolates. When we're vulnerable, we open the door for connection by demonstrating to others that they need not fear our judgment—in allowing our shame to be seen, we show them that we are capable of grace. When we're vulnerable, we signal our potential for empathy. This is what it's all about. You create the environment in which true connection can grow and in which shame finds no safe harbor.

Staying intentional helps keep us authentically vulnerable, too—it keeps the ego in check by reminding us that if we're seeking a certain outcome or response, then we're not coming from a place of true vulnerability. When we are being authentically vulnerable, we know and accept that we can't control how someone else might respond to that vulnerability—and we do it anyway. We give up control, and so, in a way, we give up power—or at least the illusion of power over how others see us. That's part of what makes it so frightening, and so hard to do. For a lot of us, trauma dumping isn't an issue—we can't be vulnerable at all, disempowered or not. The threat our shame poses is too great.

For a while, it made sense to me to describe authentic vulnerability as "empowered vulnerability" because it's the opposite state of disempowered vulnerability, or trauma dumping. But the thing is, being authentically vulnerable doesn't always feel very powerful *in the moment*. Thank you, fear. When we're authentically vulnerable, we allow our consciousness to take an unfiltered measure of reality. This unfiltered acknowledgment of your present reality is so free of pretense, so free of emotional Photoshop, so unvarnished that as you speak of it, as you say the words, you quiver, your eyes water, your throat closes, your heart tightens, your hands sweat. You're so vulnerable that it feels as close as you can get to walking outside naked.

In other words, when you're authentically vulnerable, you shed what you usually use to control how others see you; you shed what you usually use to protect yourself. We all have the impulse to protect ourselves. And sometimes we seek to protect others, too, to shield them from our truths. But when we seek to shield ourselves or others from reality, we can't be honest. And when we can't be honest, there is no opportunity for growth and connection. A shield doesn't leave room for closeness—it's literally (though metaphorically here, lol) a barrier between two people. The other thing about honesty—or the lack of it, more precisely—is that without it, there's also no possibility of being accountable to or for ourselves.

Sometimes the shame we carry with us is not about trauma we've experienced, or the ways we've learned to devalue ourselves and make ourselves small, but about harm we've done to others. I think this kind of shame is the hardest to confront for many of us because it feels the worst—harming others is deeply antisocial. It most readily risks group rejection. And it's where, morally and ethically, Shame Logic becomes most convincing. So we avoid it like hell. But avoiding the shame we feel for harming someone else also tends to mean we never do anything to repair that harm; we just carry it with us. When you carry a bag of remorse, a bag of excuses, a bag of guilt, a bag of revenge, or a bag of grudges around with you, your presence is not healing.

The truth is that unless you are utterly and profoundly, completely free, unless you are an enlightened Buddha, even if you have the purest of intentions, you will not be perfect all the time. You will hurt people. Being vulnerable enough to acknowledge that you have done so begins the process of repair, and repair helps to neutralize shame. Repair is not as hard as it sounds, but we're taught to live in shame, and that feels normal. Repair doesn't have to be a literal mending of a broken relationship or a righting of a wrong. You don't have to ask for forgiveness or make amends, per se—the person you've harmed may not welcome that, or the harm you've caused may not have had a specific target (some of us are just assholes for a while). Repair means addressing what led to the action—i.e., examining it fearlessly, learning from it, and not doing it again. You commit to stopping perpetuating harm and live by that commitment. We actually have a huge capacity to learn and repair, even in relationships in which a person is dead or no longer in our life. You can even go back across generations and find healing.

Once you actually accept that you've caused harm, you will likely feel remorse—true sadness that you've hurt someone and a feeling of being sorry for having done so—and regret—the wish that you hadn't done it (I mean, at least I hope so). Regret is sticky and tricky, though. It can cause shame to flare up again. Regret leads us back to the past, where we tend to become trapped. And people have a hard time expressing regret from a heartfelt place. Our desire to protect ourselves from shame kicks in, and defensiveness rears its head. My biggest piece of advice about repairing regrets is don't defend yourself. Just let yourself notice. Take responsibility. It's quite powerful to think of it as "I get to actually own that I had an impact on someone else. Through my words and actions, I did something that generated harm. Can I find a way to hold responsibility and respond to that without making myself bad and understand there was probably something going on? Maybe I didn't have the resources or the awareness to make a better choice at the time."

Here is the thing about regret: the choice to feel regret for what you did wrong is already a forward movement. It's not actually moving backward. If you can be vulnerable about it, then you're already propelling yourself toward growth. There have been times that I've been so overcome with regret, I have been reduced to lying on the floor. If you, like me, have felt that way, you can shift the karmic momentum of your past actions by seeing regret, as Vajrayana Buddhism suggests, as the skillful action of looking back and disentangling who you are from what you did. Realize that what's asking to die is the part of you that acted out of congruency with your Buddha nature. That is the part of you that is ready to be walked into the fire and burned to the ground so that new, more fertile ground can be cultivated. If you speak to a botanist, they'll tell you that when a forest burns down, the ashes become the most potent fertilizer. The fire actually makes the forest grow stronger, wiser, more beautiful, more lush, more green, and more fragrant. Let the forest burn itself to the ground. You're going to use those ashes. You're going to fertilize the soil of all that's good, benevolent, skillful, and holy inside you.

One of the ways you can do this is through a "regret detox." All the things that haunt you at night or in quiet moments? Write them down: *I regret that I . . .* Be honest about the things that haunt you. A regret detox requires vulnerability and bravery. Remember, bravery doesn't mean being unafraid; it means being afraid and doing it anyway. Ground yourself in the knowing that who you are right now is not the same person who did those things in the past. That's a biological and spiritual truth. The question is, are you willing to stabilize yourself in the person who you are right now? Or are you willing to continue to give power to who you were, because you're unwilling to admit that you did those things?

If you don't feel ready to confront your regrets alone with your thoughts, then you have to call your best friend or your therapist and say, "I'm gonna tell you some fucked-up shit. Can you hold it?" This is another moment where you will have to draw on your willingness to be authentically vulnerable. I know it's frightening, but if you don't have enough stable ground on your own, then you have to do it with another nervous system in front of you to help you to regulate. Otherwise, the shame and guilt that have been part of your inner lexicon and your inner dialogue will cause you to spiral.

When you name your regrets, when you write them down and read them, literally bringing them to light, you're back to learning to see in the dark, to transforming snakes into shoelaces. Your regrets can't hurt you. What you're looking at is a list of things that you no longer are, a list of things of which you don't approve. In doing so, you learn to know yourself better. You clarify your values. You clarify your boundaries. Your list of regrets becomes a map, gives you a clear path forward of all the things you won't do again. That's how you fertilize the soil. You look at the list, and you don't approve, but you do accept.

Unrepaired regrets only deepen our shame, inhibiting our connection to others. But how sad is it that the deepest regret people feel at the end of life is that they didn't spend more time with people they loved, or that they didn't foster those connections in the first place? At that moment, there's no time left to repair a regret like that. Let's take it allllll the way back to the beginning here: we need each other. There is no shame in that truth. And yet we are taught that expressing this deepest human need is a sign of weakness (it's not) and that weakness is something to be ashamed of (it's not). We need each other. And ultimately, the only way to reach others is to be real about this, to be emotionally vulnerable. Yes, there's no way around it: when you are emotionally vulnerable with another person, you risk rejection. But guess what? After the rejection, should it come, you'll still be there. "No" isn't a confirmation that you're unworthy or unlovable or that you don't belong—that you have anything to be ashamed of. Fuck shame. Write an old friend when you hear that song that reminds you of them. Tell someone you love them. Ask for help. Be vulnerable.

When we're authentically vulnerable, we can navigate pain with less suffering. That's because being vulnerable by definition means we're not resisting anything. When we wear a mask, when we work to protect ourselves, we're in control mode. When we are vulnerable, we accept that we cannot control how others perceive us, let alone life itself. When we are vulnerable, we are in a place of acceptance. Vulnerability is the gateway between two hearts. When you approach life with vulnerability about your story, your experience of being human, you invite others to see their own lives and stories in a new light and with less shame. Just by existing as yourself, without shame, you give permission to others to do so as well.

Transfiguration

When we are authentically vulnerable, we feel less shame. And when we feel less shame, acceptance—of what may have happened to us, what we may have done, how we feel, our shame itself—becomes easier to practice. In a state of acceptance, we stop resisting reality as it is. It's one of the beautiful paradoxes of life that when we stop resisting reality, when we stop arguing with the past, when we come to terms with the fact that what has been done cannot be undone—that we cannot change it—we actually create the possibility of change. We create the possibility of changing our lives moving forward, yes, but also? We actually do create the possibility of "changing the past." I know, I'm contradicting myself. But life is all about perception. What I'm speaking about here is a different, subtler, almost mystical kind of change: transfiguration.

Transfiguring your past is about changing your perception of the past. Transfiguring your past is about changing the texture of your memories, which is where the past—and the experiences it's made of—lives in the present. None of us are time travelers, but the pain and shame that reverberate outward from trauma and shame continually pull us back as if we were. To transfigure our memories ultimately means to transform their meaning, to give them new meaning, and to sanctify them. We consecrate our pain. We don't *glorify* our pain, but we understand that it is as much a part of the third truth as our joy. The third truth is about the unknown, about mystery; it is Rumi's field beyond good or bad; it's a relaxed knowing that there is harmony in chaos. The third truth reveals itself when, even in the midst of extreme, difficult times, you are able to touch your center and an overwhelming gnosis follows, washing away your resistance to reality as it is—and leaving behind new, fresh meaning, one unmediated by your conditioning, one that you are seeing for the first time. This is the power of transfiguration. When we are able to transfigure trauma, we are open to the beautiful lessons of karma. Your capacity to transfigure will inform how much compassion you are able to give and receive. If you still believe you are a bad person because of a mistake you made ten years ago, you will unknowingly stay in a cycle of hurt and therefore unconsciously create a trail of violence, propagating shame and isolation. But if you transfigure your mistake and give spiritual meaning to that experience, you'll no longer feel the need to punish yourself. You'll no longer live out a self-fulling prophecy that you are bad and you deserve bad things to happen to you. The same goes for those who have hurt you, and the hurt you feel, and the way you see them.

Slipping into abstraction is too damn seductive when talking about transfiguration, so let's bring it down to earth. When I say that transfiguration gives new meaning to our past, what's the "new meaning" that I'm talking about? The new meaning is a spiritual meaning—it's a meaning that gives us the will to keep living; it's the ability to see that "there are no mistakes in the eyes of God." Look, I'm all too aware that this verges dangerously close to "everything happens for a reason." And honestly, that is close to—but not quite—the point. "Everything happens for a reason" seems to imply that there is a logic to devastating events, and that logic is "This happened so that can happen." When my mother died, I couldn't believe how many people tried to comfort me by telling me, "Everything happens for a reason." Who wants to be told—or truly believes—that someone you loved suffered in service to . . . what? Some benefit you're going to experience down the road? Because the "reason" is by necessity supposed to be good, right? Otherwise, no one would say that. Karma is a system of cause and effect, yes. But karma is also mysterious. In the West, we tend to imagine karma as a very transparent, punitive system, but that's deeply, simply wrong. Cause and effect is not moral; it's a force affected by a multitude of impacts. And it's mysterious—humans are not the arbiters of karma; we can't always see or understand how it plays out or has played out or will play out. It extends over lifetimes, over generations.

Understanding that there are no mistakes in the eyes of God is a way of accepting life's inherent mystery. We've spent a lot of time in these pages hammering home the message that you can't argue with reality. But as concrete as reality is, it also contains the mysterious, the divine, the karmic. Accepting this mystery connects us to it, connects us to the divine, to the third truth, to what's possible. Our perspective widens. Typically, though, our view of life is very limited. We don't know what's possible, that there is possibility. We're all walking around with unprocessed pain, wearing our trauma like blinders. When you're seeing the present through the past, what are you really seeing? Not much.

Transfiguration stops us from looping in the past. Chronic oversharers, trauma dumpers, people looping in their pasts, *most of us reading this book* all operate with a strategic user error: we think that by telling our story—over and over—we'll finally make sense of it. We'll understand the *why* behind the pain, the reason. We think that by rehashing the facts of our life and running through our thoughts about those facts, we'll arrive at peace. We'll find some stabilized present-moment awareness. Sorry, honey. It's a no-go. Transfiguration happens when we process our pain, when we meet the feelings that our stories have left us with.

Transfiguration is not about assigning new meaning to every individual memory. It's not a to-do list—"Here are the seven things I have to sanctify today." You don't have to reactivate every memory in order to transfigure it; you don't have to call up your story, evoke your trauma, to heal your pain. That's where we get it wrong, and it's this misunderstanding that leads so many of us to not try or to feel defeated before we begin. Transfiguration is about focusing on the underlying feeling rather than the individual experience. Is there one moment, one quiet afternoon, where you're struck with the courage not to speak back to a negative thought and instead to let yourself really feel your anger, to really feel your sadness? For five minutes, can you choose not to leave your bed, to lie there and choose to be in the sadness? To say to yourself, "I accept that I feel sad right now; I accept that I feel angry now"? To say to yourself, "Whatever comes, let it come. Whatever goes, let it go"?

When we go toward the feelings in our body instead of talking back to our thoughts, when we can be with feelings of rejection, of blame, of shame long enough, kindly enough, patiently enough—the feelings change. They get a little lighter every time. And in that moment of change, they become less entangled with the story playing in your mind. Your entire history becomes a little less heavy because you've started to process the blame and the rejection and the fear so that all those qualities of feeling weigh less heavily through your entire biography. In this way, while it's not a one and done, the act of processing one moment does affect your entire story.

We often think that we have to heal this or that memory about this or that one person or one event and that each of these memories has different feelings associated with it. And from one side, that's real, that's true. Our relationships and experiences are specific. But if any time a painful memory surfaces, you can just be with your uncomfortable feelings in the body instead of engaging with the specifics of the story, you'll be doing the work of disentangling the two. All the times those feelings were previously activated but went unprocessed? They accumulate; they live in your body, regardless of where they originated. So you don't need to revisit the stories in your mind, or revisit the stories of your past in order to process the texture of those feelings from your biography.

Transfiguration can't be rushed. When it comes to trauma, there's no transfiguration that can happen before you have walked through the valley of shadows or crawled your way out of hell. There's no way to transfigure an experience without truly accepting that that horrible thing happened. You have to feel and experience the pain of it. If you shut it away, there's no transfiguration. At my mother's funeral, a lot of people approached me to tell me she was in a better place because she had been suffering. They weren't wrong, exactly. But you can't force transfiguration down someone's throat as trauma is happening. You can't transfigure the funeral of your mother as it's taking place. Let me go through the grief, the mourning, the terror, the dissolution, the disorientation, the crumbling—give me time to arrive at the fact that it happened. Transfiguration requires you to walk through the fire.

Traumas themselves are transfiguring. More times than I can count, someone has told me they wish they could go back to who they were before the trauma, that they wish they could be the person they were before the pain. This is a lost cause. Yes, trauma changes us, but pain is inevitable, and you don't really know who you would have been if it hadn't happened. Dwelling on who you would have been or how you would be different or how your life would be different is just another form of resistance, adding suffering to pain. And it's a rejection of the self. You wouldn't be who you are now without the trauma; you would be someone different. Part of transfiguration is the grace that allows you to embrace that, to embrace rather than reject yourself. Trauma is a fact of life; everyone is going to go through it. Choosing to transfigure it means you're choosing to let go of how you have let it define you. And when you sanctify the memory, give it new meaning, the meaning only has to be "Okay, this horrible thing happened. I survived it. I'm connected to the will to live in a more meaningful and deeper way." That's enough.

Shame is all about certainty: the certainty that we are unworthy, inadequate, fundamentally broken. Transfiguration is about gnosis, and it's about the unknown, what could be, on the other side of shame. When you give spiritual meaning to your past, you move past ideas of good and bad. Try as we might to intellectualize it with the mind, this is the work of the heart, which speaks through intuition, silence, synchronicity, and life communicating back to you. Stop, pause, and breathe. Make space to allow revelation to come in—those new understandings, those new ways of seeing, those moments where you suddenly know something you don't know how you know. Something you've only glimpsed out of the corner of your eye coming into focus. Something concealed laid bare. That's where revelation and vulnerability meet—in the space where we meet the world and the world meets us, unveiled, unobscured, unscreened, without shame.

Chapter 7

The Karma of It All

On the twenty-seventh night of a thirty-day silent retreat in Kathmandu, Nepal, I had what was—and remains—both the most vivid and most frightening dream of my life. In it, I watched, disembodied, as I hung myself, naked, from the ceiling of the Gompa, the room where we meditated and received teachings every day. With horror, I saw the other students enter the Gompa, discovering my nude and lifeless body suspended in its center.

The four weeks leading up to this had been some of the most difficult of my life. Seven months earlier, I'd done my first retreat in India, only a few months after slinking out of New York in shame. *That* retreat had been beyond revelatory: in it, in learning about impermanence, I had faced the inevitability of my own death for the first time and started coming to terms with my own mortality. That was also when I'd encountered the nun who had introduced me to the idea of innate goodness, been told that all of us—including *me*—possess this basic goodness. Awakening to these truths, gaining that awareness, had been deeply healing and inspiring. Yes, I had started having to integrate memories and process my feelings in a way I'd previously avoided, but it was all enveloped in excitement about what was possible for me going forward. My time was limited, but that made it valuable, and I was good—I deserved to learn and grow and set out on the path of liberation.

This second retreat? Not so much. At its outset, I didn't really understand yet that I *couldn't be liberated* unless I faced my darkness, until I integrated my shadows. And that was what the next four weeks turned out to be all about—focusing our lovingkindness on our shame; shining its light on the aspects of ourselves we hated, the mistakes we had made, all the things we had done and that were done to us that caused harm. As Pema Chödrön said, and I'm paraphrasing here, unless you have met your own darkness, you can't be with the darkness of others. That's what we were learning to do: know our own darkness, our own suffering, so that we could be *present* for the darkness, the suffering of others. So we could learn to practice true compassion.

It was as if I had suddenly hit "play" on a reel of my worst moments. I was flooded with all the ways I had hurt other people and all the ways other people had hurt me. Not only was I unprepared for this, but I was also angry and afraid. I hadn't asked to be flooded with my unprocessed past. Previously, I had done a great job of disassociating and distracting myself anytime memories like those popped up, anytime those feelings popped up, demanding to be processed. It was as if the retreat had flipped a switch on my night vision, though, and it was activated now whether I liked it or not. I couldn't help but see the trauma cluttering my inner world. And because I didn't yet have the tools to process my feelings in my body, I felt physically sick most of the time.

It didn't help that I could literally not talk to anybody about any of this. We had a brief break in the afternoons when we were allowed to speak, but because this time was so abbreviated, it was hard to develop the kind of intimacy that made it feel possible to discuss anything with virtual strangers. We barely had time to get to know each other. I was alone with myself and had nowhere to run. In meditation, we are tasked with observing without evaluation. But outside practice, it was incredibly hard to stay present, to concentrate, to settle in myself. Facing my own shit meant accepting that I had lived in a way that I wasn't proud of, but it also meant realizing that I had been my own worst enemy. There was a lot of sorrow that came with that.

Hard truth arrived with disturbing clarity: I could now see that every painful experience I had had, I had made worse than it was in my mind. When someone had done something to me, I had made it worse in my mind. When I had done something harmful to another person, I had made it worse in my mind. That was really alarming to me: I couldn't trust myself—my mind did not process facts; it processed a narrative about those facts that was conditioned, indoctrinated, *poisoned*.

The Three Poisons

In Buddhism, a central tenet of practice is that all humans are afflicted with three character flaws: attachment, aversion, and ignorance, which together are called "the three poisons." These flaws don't negate our inner goodness, but they sure as shit make it harder to touch and are at the root of the craving—the grasping—that causes suffering.

Think of attachment as greed, as it is often translated in this context. Put simply, whatever feels good, we want to hold on to, hoard it, as we know. We exaggerate the deliciousness of it. But also, whatever feels good? We want *more* of it. We adapt to how things are; shiny things lose their luster through handling. Attachment traps us in a cycle of constant craving. In this unsustainable cycle, nothing and no one will ever be good enough. Contentment is not possible.

Aversion has two other faces: hatred and aggression. Just as we are drawn to what makes us happy, brings us pleasure, and sustains the illusion of the self-as-fixed-identity (as opposed to the self-as-ongoing-process), we have an aversion to anything we don't like, anything we hate, anything that threatens the ego or our survival. With aversion, we avoid all things even remotely uncomfortable and buy in totally to the fiction of duality: aversion locks us into judgment and into seeing difference as otherness, seeing people with whom we don't identify as The Other. And because we are willing to hurt The Other to protect the self, aversion leads to violence.

Ignorance involves a lack of understanding of the impermanent and interconnected nature of all things. This ignorance gives rise to a sense of inherent existence and a belief in a separate and independent self.

Ignorance also leads to a misunderstanding of the law of cause and effect—karma. When we are not guided by ignorance, we have knowing of the true nature of reality, including the concepts of impermanence, nonself (the absence of an independently existing self), and interdependence. Ignorance is the result and source of attachment and aversion. It's the belief that someone or something is either for me or against me, and if they are neither, they don't matter. It is ignorance of our shared humanity, and therefore also an indifference to our shared humanity. Ignorance is a type of delusion: the delusion of separateness. Me and them. It's the devotion to the belief that happiness is found outside ourselves; when we grasp, we reinforce the notion that there is a "me" to do the grasping and a "them" or an object to be grasped—between us lies separation.

We call these three flaws "the three poisons" because they poison our perception of reality. They pollute our system. They cloud our mind and cause us to take actions—to create karma—that are harmful. The three poisons fuck with our intentions—the *why* behind what we do, the *cause* of action—and, as you know by now, intentions are everything: they lead to how we move through the world and what happens to us. In other words, when any of the poisons motivate our thoughts and behaviors, we will suffer in the form of karma.

Ask yourself: how much of any given day, how much of your *life*, is is driven by one or more of these three poisons? Ignorance is probably the most difficult to recognize in ourselves (you don't know what you don't know), but attachment and aversion are easier to spot. Once you identify them, you can tease out the ignorance that is their root cause. Be honest but gentle with yourself here—it's not that *you* are ignorant per se, but that we're all caught in a state of samsaric amnesia until we reach liberation. In Buddhism, "samsara" means the endless cycle of birth, death, and rebirth that is characterized by suffering. It's the forgetfulness that we are born with Buddha nature, innately good; that we're not separate; that binary dualities and the perception of self-as-fixed-identity are *misperceptions*. The thing is, even knowing all this, it's still so damn hard to really sense the poisons at work when we're operating solo. But if you explore this in the context of relationship with others, it becomes truly eye-opening how the poisons course through your thoughts and intentions. So many of us are hooked in a push-pull pattern of I like you, I hate you; I love you, I hate you; I want you, go away; you're mine, get lost. What we love the most becomes something that poisons us.

Personally, coming to grips with the three poisons—how I had given them free rein over my life, and the karma I had sown—really shook me. From one side, this should have been a huge weight off my shoulders, a release, a long *aaaaaaaaah*. Now that I could see what was burdening me—now that I knew I was even shouldering a burden—I could set it down, right? But from the other side, it wasn't so simple. I couldn't just set this burden down. It was more like I was carrying a yoke than a bundle, and one side of the yoke supported a full bucket of poison and the other an empty bucket. There was nothing to offset the weight. I was off balance. Walking the path without filling the other bucket would be impossible. In order to restore balance, I would have to fill that empty bucket with the antidotes to the poisons. I would have to commit to the ongoing work of undoing my conditioning.

Taking Refuge

Ah, commitment. Let's hit that *rewind* button for a sec. Take it back to, oh, just there. Perfect. Stop. It's the night of my dream. Maybe I should have mentioned that the night I had the dream followed the day that I was formally invited to *take refuge*, the commitment ceremony that—if I chose to participate—would officially make me a Buddhist.

The morning after the dream, I found myself fixating on its symbolism and interpreting it as a sign that I should not take refuge. Not only should I not take refuge, in fact, I should run out of the monastery gates, down the hill to town, catch the next taxi to the airport, and jump on whatever flight would take me home as quickly as possible. After all, who could argue with this dream? It had to be a portent, and an ominous one at that, right? I killed myself in the meditation room: this path was a danger to me. I was naked: this path meant exposure, and exposure must also mean danger. I was discovered by other students: attempting belonging in this community would only cause further shame.

At teatime that afternoon, sitting with one of the only other students I had managed to forge some connection with, I confessed my dream—and my doubts. Sydney, my kind and generous friend, listened calmly and with remarkable presence. I felt seen, and more importantly, I didn't feel judged. When I had finished talking, Sydney sat quietly for a few beats. Then she suggested that maybe this path *was* a danger to me—the *part* of me that was dying and didn't want to let go. "The part of you that's dying *is* scared," she said. "If you take refuge, eventually, it will be gone for good."

What she said landed the way only the truth can. We all recognize the texture of truth; we have all felt the "click" when understanding is unlocked by revelation. The truth was, I was scared of how rapidly I was transforming, how rapidly and inexorably I was getting to know my shadow, and I was scared of entering the darkness and making friends with it. Some part of me—the part that got to avoid my intolerable feelings, the part that got to shove down the shame, la-di-da, and flounce around pretending I was fine—*was* going to die if I continued on this path, and I didn't want that. The part of me that was dying was the part of me that was afraid of being exposed, of being seen by others for who I was, no carefully crafted costume in place to cloak me. It was the part that knew that when I took refuge, none of those things would be an option anymore. Committing to the path of liberation meant committing to confronting my darkness, integrating it, sharing myself with others, and allowing myself to be seen. Was I really ready?

That night, I chose to take refuge. Doing so was a leap of faith. Even as I jumped, I wobbled, though. After the ceremony was over, I left the monastery, headed for the small cluster of shops just beyond its boundary. In one of them, I bought a pack of cigarettes. I returned to the monastery and hiked up to the summit of a sacred hill, where I proceeded to chain smoke almost the entire pack. The night was so cold, cold in the way that seems to make scents sharper and stars brighter. I can still smell those Nepalese cigarettes to this day: sweet but harsh, a whiff almost of incense in the smoke. The blue Patagonia windbreaker I was wearing—which, somehow, is still hanging in the back of my closet after all these years—was not up for the job, but I sat there anyway, shivering and smoking, thinking about what I had done.

What does it mean to take refuge? And if I was searching for refuge, did that make me a refugee? To me, a refuge meant a safe place, somewhere to take shelter. You sought refuge—you were a refugee—if you needed to escape danger, to escape suffering. I had been suffering for years, and I *was* in danger: in danger of losing myself to my pain. Those things I had sought to numb the pain, that I had sought refuge in? Status, approval, the next best high? None of them had given me relief, none of them had offered true shelter. None of them were lasting.

In Buddhism, when you take refuge, you quite literally vow to take refuge in the Buddha, the dharma, and the sangha, also known as "the Three Jewels." Three times, you recite, "I take refuge in the Buddha. I take refuge in the dharma. I take refuge in the sangha." It's said that the traditions around and language of the refuge vows have been passed down from Buddha to teacher to student in an unbroken lineage for over 2,500 years, so much so that it's as if you're committing yourself at the feet of the Buddha himself. Talk about pressure, honey. Added to that, there's a way in which taking refuge has a certain finality to it. The jig is up; you're admitting that the only path to liberation lies within, and there's no other way. Taking the vow, I really felt the weight of the words and all they implied: that I would have to let go of all my old habits and work continuously to become the most liberated version of myself so that I could better help to liberate others. The commitment sat heavy on my heart as I smoked and wondered if I really had what it takes.

But as I sat turning over each vow in my mind, I felt a sense of peace. Taking refuge in the Buddha was to take refuge in the potential for my own liberation. It meant taking refuge in my own awakened awareness—I could learn to trust myself again. It meant honoring the Buddha nature that already existed within me. Dharma means teachings—the Buddha's teachings—but it also symbolizes a path: the path of those teachings, the path of *learning*. When we take refuge in the path of dharma, we take refuge in the experience of being a student, and we understand that *whatever* we encounter while walking the path presents an opportunity for wisdom to emerge. I didn't have to be perfect. I just had to practice. I was committing to developing my awareness so that I could help other people develop theirs. And I wouldn't have to—I couldn't—do it alone.

Sangha, the third jewel, means community. Traditionally, this means the community of other Buddhists—those who, like you, are on the path. Sangha speaks to a deep companionship, a sharing of values. Like you, the people in your sangha are alert to their darkness and working to meet it. They're not paralyzed with fear of what lurks in the dark. They're walking the path with you, offering feedback about and reference points for our progress on that path. We learn from them, and we learn about ourselves from them—the sangha is the loving mirror reflecting back to us what's working and what's not. And yes, I took refuge in knowing my community of like-minded seekers would be there to inspire me, to teach me, and to fuel my own capacity for teaching and inspiring in kind—for practicing lovingkindness and being compassionate. But sitting there under the limitless night sky, I felt a deep sense of gratitude when I thought about the sangha waiting for me—and that I could foster—beyond the monastery walls, beyond Zen centers and dharma workshops, in the mess of everyday life. Those people who would ride the waves with me, without whom not only could I not do life, but all my spiritual practices would mean nothing. My sacred friends.

Creating Sangha

You, my love, are part of my sangha now. We may not have met, but in writing this book and in reading this book, we've been in conversation about the things that matter most. And here, as we reach the end of the book, I want to say thank you for letting me join you on this part of your path. As I wrote this book, I remembered, I felt in my body the resistance I've felt at different times during my own (ongoing) journey. And I expect you've felt resistance, too, reading this. Maybe it was resistance to the very premise of this book: we need each other. Maybe it was resistance to the idea that we all possess inner goodness. Maybe it was resistance to acceptance, or forgiveness, or the possibility of transfiguration. Maybe it was resistance to believing that your shame doesn't need to be a life sentence. That connection is possible for all of us. Whatever it was or is, sacred friendship doesn't require you to "get over" your resistance to starting to be a sacred friend. You don't have to be perfect at loving yourself or anyone else radically at all times, to be compassionate without fail. All sacred friendship requires is a commitment to trying—to practice.

It would be disingenuous not to acknowledge that many of us are, for whatever reason, in a season where we may not have a ton of friends. Or not to acknowledge that the older we get, the harder it is to make new friends. When I first conceived of this book, it had a little more of a "how to" vibe: how to be magnetic, how to attract friendship. Pretty quickly, that started to feel a little icky . . . a little too much in the realm of personal development and far, far from spirituality. With "how to make friends," there seemed to be an inescapable undercurrent of manipulation—how do I make someone else like me?—and, shudder, of manifestation.

Manifestation is pretend spirituality for capitalists. *Damnnnnnnn.* Was that tea too hot, honey? Honestly, I'll serve it again, piping hot, anytime. Manifestation is everything that's wrong with what people call spirituality now. It's a me-focused attempt to manipulate the universe so that we get a desired outcome. It's the definition of craving and grasping. It's why I tell my students to pray for a miracle instead of an outcome. A miracle is never what you want. It's always something bigger, something much more profound. It's unexpected and takes you outside your comfort zone. Personal development, meanwhile, is about creating safety for the ego. Liberation is the opposite. It's like that quotation attributed to Chögyam Trungpa Rinpoche: "The bad news is you're falling through the air, nothing to hang on to, no parachute. The good news is there's no ground." Life is ongoing change. We can spend our energy on panic, on trying to manipulate outcomes, or we can relax into the freefall—the relentlessness of impermanence—and realize there is no danger. So, yeah: I didn't want to write about making friends.

Here's the other side of that. I *am* writing about making friends—because I'm writing about how to treat people, including ourselves. You can't make friends (or at least keep them) if you don't know how to *be* a friend. At the most basic level, when we treat people well, with love and without the expectation of anything in return, they tend to want to be friends. We attract friendship when we are present, when we are curious, when we are trustworthy, when we are inspirational, when we refrain from judgment, when we see people's inner goodness. We attract friendship when we can be at ease with other people's shadows, because we have met our own.

And we attract friendship when we bring what we've learned to strangers. Sangha isn't just what you have, it's what you build. Move beyond your echo chamber, seek out connection with people different from you. Know that the work you've been doing throughout this book isn't meant to apply only to your core five, your inner circle—or even to your backyard BBQ 15 or your weddings and funerals 150. It's meant to guide how you interact with all people. Being "Spiritually, We" isn't just about your existing social groups. It's about how do I bring that energy to the world? How do I drive in traffic like that? How do I shop at Whole Foods like that?

Anyone can sell you strategies for how to meet people—attracting friendship is about an orientation toward life. I *am* writing about making friends—because I'm writing about how to walk the path of liberation. And walking the path of liberation leads to a magnetic personality—it draws friendship to you. It's the karma of it all.

We need each other. Our wellness depends on it. And so does our liberation. We can't get free alone. That's the spiritual equation we've been talking about from the beginning: fifty percent of the work takes place between you and you, but the other fifty percent takes place between you and your community. The deep power in a "Spiritually, We" orientation toward life, though, is that we not only possess the ability to liberate each other but also have the potential to liberate the world. The truly amazing equation, though? It doesn't take all of us. It doesn't even take a lot of us. If only two percent of people committed to becoming and living as sacred friends, we could shift the consciousness of all people everywhere.

The Possibility of Healing the World

We are trained to see science and spirituality as fundamentally opposed, and yet some of our most rigorous scientists are also our most spiritual. Dr. Lisa Miller, the founder of Columbia University's Spirituality Mind Body Institute—the first Ivy League graduate program and research institute in spirituality and psychology—with whom I spoke earlier about the limiting perspectives with which we view each other (and which cause us to relate transactionally rather than with love), has done extensive research on the transformative effects of spirituality on the brain.

In her work, Dr. Miller has, amazingly, demonstrated a physiological foundation for spirituality, revealing that our brains are wired for it and that the part of our brain that perceives our relationship to spirit is the same part that perceives intimacy and connection with each other; in other words, *love*. When we perceive people with love, we are, in Dr. Miller's language, perceiving them as "a soul on earth" rather than a mechanical assemblage of parts. Love, connection, and spirituality—and our awareness of them, our ability to perceive them—share the same neural circuitry.

What's so fascinating to me is that Dr. Miller's findings also demonstrate that people who regularly engage in spiritual practice have a thicker cerebral cortex than those who do not. As Dr. Miller writes in her book *The Awakened Brain*, "The cerebral cortex is where we process emotional stimuli. Specifically, this part of the brain is important to reasoning, planning, and mood. A thinner cortex inhibits our ability to perceive and orient in the world, and see ourselves clearly."[1] So a thicker cortex helps us with accurate perception, and people who rate themselves as highly spiritual have a thicker cortex. But what Dr. Miller found is that this isn't just some fixed genetic trait—we can *actively* thicken the cerebral cortex through spiritual practice, regardless of how spiritual we are to begin with. We can actively thicken the cerebral cortex through a perception of each other as souls on earth.

When we practice seeing people this way day in and day out, we develop cortical thickness. In a sense, then, developing the capacity to perceive each other this way is like building a muscle—it's a strength we can build. The more we do it, the more it becomes our go-to, our default perception. The brain can be trained, but we have to teach it. Does it require special training to see people as spiritual beings? No, it requires love. Love is the practice. When you love people radically, when you see their inherent divinity, their holiness, their *basic goodness*, you come closer to liberation.

What does this have to do with healing the world? Well, the more that scholars and researchers study consciousness—in other words, awareness and perception—the closer together science and spirituality come. It's wild, but from physicists to neuroscientists, a portrait of consciousness is emerging that reveals consciousness as a field—for each of us, our self-awareness, our experience of consciousness, is actually just one part of that field. In spiritual terms? Each of us is a vessel for consciousness rather than its source.

Why does this matter? Because it points to consciousness as nonlocal, and nonlocality explains the mystery of entanglement—the phenomenon, as observed by quantum physics, of two particles affecting each other even across vast distances. We can affect each other's consciousness across great distances because we are participating in one field of consciousness. We are entangled. It is our awareness, our attention and perception, that affects the field of consciousness. In a sense, as we take the measure of reality, we necessarily affect it.

Perception is a choice, and our perception affects the field of consciousness. All along, throughout *Spiritually, We*, we've been talking about training our perception. Dr. Miller's work shows us that this kind of training can actively change our brains and that perception can become habitual. So what would it mean for the field of consciousness if a "Spiritually, We" orientation toward life become our default mode of awareness?

In our conversation, Dr. Miller introduced me to the term "entrainment." Entrainment describes the action of two oscillations becoming synchronized. A pendulum is a great example of oscillation: it swings back and forth regularly at the same pace, always from the same central point. If two pendulums were to begin to swing at the same tempo, they would be entrained. In the late 1980s, scientists began studying the possibility of brain wave entrainment between people. Going forward, numerous studies using electroencephalogram (EEG) testing—which measures electrical activity in the brain—showed entrainment between two people who were empathetically connected: people who meditated together, people who mirrored each other on a task, people who prayed together. Their brain waves' oscillations synchronized. The effects of entrainment grew even stronger when larger numbers of people joined together. As Dr. Miller wrote, "People who pray together . . . accelerate the rate at which fellow worshippers activate neuropathways of a prayerful state. And it's as though the spiritual state is not only shared but also contagious. If nine people are praying together, their brains are entrained, and when a tenth person enters the room, the newcomer quickly arrives at the same entrained, spiritual state."[2]

We are all just vessels for consciousness. When we choose to come together and perceive each other from an empathic state—when we join in sacred friendship—we can entrain the consciousness of those around us, and we can, eventually, change the consciousness field of the world. It is loving, sacred consciousness itself that is transformative. Even if you come into a room and don't say a word, know that you are a conduit of consciousness; the energy is in you, but you must choose its frequency. You must actively come back when you're in judgment, when you're in separation, when you're in criticism, when you're in gossip—anytime you feel one of the three poisons polluting your thoughts. At those moments, it's time to take a breath and come back to your body, whisper a mantra, realign your perspective. Remind yourself that we are all an expression of spirit.

We are an open system. If each person lives truly and fully and expressively as a conduit, as a channel of spirit, and all those around them are touched—since spirit is much more powerful than whatever people walk in the door with—how many people who are on the path to freedom would we need in order to entrain the consciousness of the entire world? Is it possible to shift the consciousness of the whole world? Yes. And it could take as few as two out of every one hundred people to do so.

The Princeton Engineering Anomalies Research (PEAR) lab was founded in 1979 by Robert G. Jahn, a professor of aerospace engineering and dean of the School of Engineering and Applied Science at Princeton University, to study the ability of consciousness to influence physical processes. For years, pilots had been describing to Dr. Jahn a "ghost in the machine," a sense that their planes were either conscious or responded to consciousness. Because Dr. Jahn was an engineer, and what pilots were describing could in theory affect flight safety—you know, whether planes go up or down—he felt that he couldn't ignore them. He spent thirty to forty years conducting tightly controlled experiments, especially around random-number-generating machines. Volunteers would come into the lab and be asked to convey, with their heart and consciousness, an intention for the numbers on the random-number-generating machine to go up—and the mean number would increase. And then, with the same person and same machine, they'd be asked to drive the mean down. The lab found that the more connected people were, the more they would impact the inanimate machine, which is to say that it's we as people who are vessels of consciousness, and consciousness is highly transformative—it can even change the physical world.

Dr. Jahn reviewed the results of thousands of experiments using the same or similar setups. And it took only two percent of people applying their conscious intention to shift the numbers. The Maharishi effect shows similar impacts through transcendental meditation. In 1960, Maharishi Mahesh Yogi predicted that if just one percent of the global population practiced transcendental meditation, the entire world would experience a greater—and measurably so—quality of life. In 1993, as part of an experiment to test this hypothesis, four thousand people gathered in Washington, DC, and meditated intentionally. What followed was an over ten percent drop in crime, without any other observable reasons. Different experiments have produced different numbers. The real takeaway is that doesn't have to be all of us. And given that, each one of us who chooses to be "Spiritually, We" matters quite a bit. Matters a lot.

We can heal the world. We can create karma that attracts sacred friendship. And the more of us there are living like this, working toward our own and each other's liberation, the more rapidly we can transform our culture, our old, broken ways of thinking and being that only generate isolation and loneliness, that keep us stuck in our conditioning and suffering. We don't have to be afraid of the darkness. The more light we shed on our inner darkness, the more light we are able to offer others. Together, we light the path for the world.

Conclusion

Writing this book has been a two-year odyssey. During this time I had to navigate some really fucking rough terrain, a landscape I never thought I'd have to cross so soon: the death of my mother. There is no uplifting moral to this story, no "silver lining," as much as I wish there were. But there were surprises. None greater than the fact that, even as I was flattened by searing unhappiness, I still felt flashes of joy. They were fleeting, and they didn't exactly lessen my pain—but those flashes did, however briefly, illuminate the darkness. Those pinpoints of light, of joy, kept me from losing my way entirely.

Joy is always available in the present moment. Most of us don't realize this, though, because we mistake happiness—which is largely circumstantial—for joy, which is an ongoing state of being. And because joy lives in presence, accessing it is near impossible in a world obsessed with distraction. We find so much refuge in distraction. Our phones are distraction heroin. Future tripping, past looping: both distraction. Don't get me wrong, now—the last thing a true mama's boy like me wants after their mama leaves this plane is presence. Gimme all the distraction from this fucking pain. Even with my years of practice, with my teaching: Give. It. To. Me.

So, where did the joy sneak in? In connection. As I floundered around in the twilight aftermath of my mom's death, so many people extended not just a hand, but *their* presence. They focused their loving consciousness on me, entraining *my* presence. They brought me to the present moment. The foundation of a decade of practice meant that even during this bleak as shit time—maybe especially during this time—once there, I was often able to stay there, to feel the feelings move through me, and to experience, on the other side of them, joy. Not all the time, not even for long stretches of time, but it was undeniably there. I didn't feel good, no. Obviously. But I felt *okay*. That okayness was my lifeline to the world. And that's what joy is: serenity.

After my mom's death, I started training in a clinical pastoral education program at a hospital here in Los Angeles. My mom died in a hospital and the lack of support our family experienced there added so much suffering to our pain. Becoming a chaplain felt like a natural extension of my bodhisattva vows—my commitment as a Buddhist to make alleviating the suffering of others my life's work—and of my reverence for my mother. And there has been so much joy in it, so much more than I expected. Doing this work has demonstrated the profound truth of the folk wisdom that "joy shared is doubled, sorrow shared is halved."

It's hard though: the four pillars of the chaplain's role are working with patients and families to restore hope, connection, meaning and purpose. The hope piece has been tricky for me—I have had to resist the impulse to "offer hope," even though I should know better. You're meant to hear what patients say and reflect it back to them—to offer connection, to be the mirror through which they learn something about themselves. That's where the hope emerges, in the learning, in the revelation. Trying to resolve or fix or offer hope as a way to distract a patient from their pain does them a disservice. Because of course it does—it robs them of the present.

My mentor, Rabbi Sarah Barukh, always reminds me: you are the cookie, you don't need to bring a cookie into the room. You are the cookie? She means *your presence is the offering*. Surprise—even I need reminding of that. When it comes down to it, my job is to be a sacred friend. To be present. To reject distraction. To just be with discomfort. To offer the opportunity for joy. Even if it's just a flash, just a pinprick of light. And we can only arrive at joy once our senses aren't grasping on to gratification, once we release the need to hear nice things, see nice things, smell nice things, taste nice things, do nice things to be happy. Once we're not circumstantially hooked.

There is nothing wrong with happiness, my darling. Of course not! Time and again we say right here in these pages that we want to support others to be happy. In this life, there is plenty of room for things working out in your favor. There's room for the best case scenario. But if those are the only times you're "happy," you've missed the plot. So, if there's one thing I want you to know as you turn the last page of this book and shut its cover, it's that *joy* is always there for you in the present moment. And that connection brings us there like nothing else.

Acknowledgments

This book is a tribute to my beautiful mother, Patricia De Simone Ayoub, who taught me how to love unconditionally. I understand connection because of her, my first connection, and it is one that will never wane, wherever her beautiful spirit resides. Our connection is ancient, it's not worldly, it's not from this lifetime. My mother had a profound ability to connect to the world from a "Spiritually, We" place, warming whatever room she entered with her brilliant smile and contagious enthusiasm for life. Though my heart was broken as I wrote, my grief opened me up to a deeper understanding of just how much we need each other. Thank you, mama—for the wisdom, for the joy—for everything. I love you forever.

To my father, whose 40-year marriage to my mother modeled for me what a true soul connection, animated by radical love and compassion, should look like, and who walked with me, literally side by side in grief for 500 miles, restoring me to sanity. Thank you for your courage, your kindness, your gentleness, and your unshakable love.

To my older sister, Moun, my best friend of many lifetimes. From day one, you have always taken care of me. Thank you for your unconditional love and for teaching me it is safe to be vulnerable: even when I've been terrified, you have never been afraid of my darkness. Thank you for letting in the light.

To my little brother, Micky, my toughest critic but firmest ally. Thank you for always being honest, for your epic ability to speak truth in a single word.

To my dear friend and colleague, Libby Edelson, for picking me up when I was down, inspiring me when I was lacking inspiration, pushing me to my edges, challenging me to go deeper, and moving me to bring the best that I have to offer. Thank you for the support, for being the game changer that has made any of this possible. You are an oracle, someone who can peer through and see between the layers, and give words to things that don't have words. Your ability to communicate the ineffable in such pristine and prolific ways so that we can hear them is a true gift.

To my agent, Coleen O'Shea, for keeping me in check and on track, always with a loving but firm hand and complete lack of BS. Thank you for shepherding my literary career with such care and integrity.

To my editor, Diana Ventimiglia, for believing in me and always understanding my vision, and for advocating for me time and time again. Thank you for your patience and your commitment to this book.

To the entire Sounds True team, with special gratitude to Jaime Schwalb, Angela Wix, and Alan Getto. Thank you so much for bringing your remarkable passion, talent, and sensitivity to every stage of this project. I am beyond lucky to be able to publish with you.

To Kim Burns, for keeping it all together. Thank you for warding off disaster, for being so conscientious and so diligent, for dealing with my crazy, and doing it with such warmth and good cheer. You are a true gem.

To Dana LaRue Park, a word witch with the power to translate my chaos into beautiful, impactful language that connects. Thank you for always being in my corner and for your instrumental role in getting this book off the ground.

To Benjamin W. Decker, thank you for being one of my first readers, for helping me stay focused on the book when I wanted to do anything but, and for your generous insights and feedback.

To Melissa Valentine, thank you for supporting the initial phase of this journey and for saying yes to the ride for as long as you could.

Huge gratitude to all the people I am lucky to call my friends— you epitomize what this book is about—with a special shout out to Tiffany Kappeler, Mia Magik, Lyle Maxson; Shannon Algeo; Adriana

Rizzolo; Alexandra Roxo; Ruby Warrington; Ashley Elizabeth; Maria Francisca, Kerri Kelly; Ian Daniel; Sahara Rose; Diego Perez; Lisa Levine, Jackie Cantwell; Luca Renzi; Tashi Choedup; Devi Brown; Vikain Hanounik; Vandana Hart; Jennifer Sodini; Kate Shela; Josefina Bashout; KYMÅ; Gabriel Marques; Lisa Marie Schneider, Harshada Wagner, and Ansley Weller.

To my cherished mentors, the Venerable Tenzin Chogkyi, the Venerable Sarah Thresher, and the Venerable Joan Nicell—my heart brims with immeasurable appreciation. Their guidance has not only illuminated the sacred path of dharma but has also shone as beacons of humanity's highest potential.

To the many ridiculously intelligent, pioneering, and compassionate scientists, doctors, researchers, and teachers I spoke with about everything from loneliness to addiction to forgiveness to the brain-on-spirituality, including Dr. Lisa Miller, Dr. Rachel Wurzman, Kristin Masters, and Rachel Pringle, thank you for giving so generously of your time and for sharing your reliance and hard earned wisdom and insights so freely. I am in awe of your brilliance.

Notes

Chapter 1: We Need Each Other

1. Tim Adams, "John Cacioppo: 'Loneliness Is Like an Iceberg—It Goes Deeper than We Can See,'" *Guardian*, February 28, 2016, theguardian.com/science/2016/feb/28/loneliness-is-like-an-iceberg -john-cacioppo-social-neuroscience-interview.

2. National Academies of Sciences, Engineering, and Medicine, "Social Isolation and Loneliness in Older Adults: Opportunities for the Health Care System" (Washington, DC: National Academies Press, 2020), xi, 1, 17–18, 53, 55, 60, 104; A. Stravynski and R. Boyer, "Loneliness in Relation to Suicide Ideation and Parasuicide: A Population-Wide Study," *Suicide and Life-Threatening Behavior* 31 (2001): 32–40; A. R. Rich and R. L. Bonner, "Concurrent Validity of a Stress-Vulnerability Model of Suicidal Ideation and Behavior: A Follow-Up Study," *Suicide and Life-Threatening Behavior* 17 (1987): 265–270.

3. David A. Reinhard, Sara H. Konrath, William D. Lopez, and Heather G. Cameron, "Expensive Egos: Narcissistic Males Have Higher Cortisol," *PLOS ONE*, January 23, 2012, journals.plos.org/ plosone/article?id=10.1371/journal.pone.0030858.

4. Richard Weissbourd, Milena Batanova, Virginia Lovison, and Eric Torres, "Loneliness in America: How the Pandemic Has Deepened an Epidemic of Loneliness and What We Can Do About It," Harvard Graduate School of Education, Making Caring Common Project, February 2021, mcc.gse.harvard.edu/reports/loneliness-in -america.

5. "New Cigna Study Reveals Loneliness at Epidemic Levels in America," May 1, 2018, prnewswire.com/news-releases/new-cigna -study-reveals-loneliness-at-epidemic-levels-in-america-300639747 .html; "Cigna U.S. Loneliness Index: Survey of 20,000 Americans Examining Behaviors Driving Loneliness in the United States," May 2018, multivu.com/players/English/8294451-cigna-us -loneliness-survey/docs/IndexReport_1524069371598-173525450 .pdf.

6. Holly Hedegaard, Sally C. Curtin, and Margaret Warner, "Suicide Rates in the United States Continue to Increase," NCHS Data Brief No. 309, June 2018, cdc.gov/nchs/data/databriefs/db309.pdf.

7. Interviews with Dr. Rachel Wurzman, video calls, February 24 and April 25, 2022.

8. Pema Chödrön, *When Things Fall Apart*, 20th anniversary ed. (Boulder, CO: Shambhala, 2016), 34–35.

9. Bastiaan T. Heijmans, Elmar W. Tobi, Aryeh D. Stein, Hein Putter, Gerard J. Blauw, Ezra S. Susser, P. Eline Slagboom, and L. H. Lumey, "Persistent Epigenetic Differences Associated with Prenatal Exposure to Famine in Humans," *Proceedings of the National Academy of Sciences of the United States of America* 105, no. 44 (November 2008): 17046–17049, ncbi.nlm.nih.gov/pmc/articles/ PMC2579375/.

10. Dalai Lama, *How to Practice: The Way to a Meaningful Life*, ed. and trans. Jeffrey Hopkins (New York: Simon and Schuster, 2002), 66.

Chapter 2: Sacred Friendship

1. Lydia Denworth, *Friendship: The Evolution, Biology, and Extraordinary Power of Life's Fundamental Bond* (New York: W. W. Norton, 2020), 12, 247.

Chapter 3: Be a Spiritual Gardener

1. Rumi, *The Essential Rumi*, trans. Coleman Barks and John Moyne (New York: HarperCollins, 1995).

2. "Tenzin Palmo Jetsunma—the Difference between Genuine Love and Attachment," YouTube, June 12, 2016, youtube.com/watch?v=6kUoTS3Yo4g&t=66s.

3. Valerie Kaur, *See No Stranger: A Memoir and Manifesto of Revolutionary Love* (New York: One World, 2020), 23.

Chapter 4: Conflict Is for Lovers

1. C. G. Jung, *Memories, Dreams, Reflections*, rec. and ed. Aniela Jaffe, trans. Richard and Clara Winston, reissue ed. (New York: Vintage Books, 1989), 521.

2. Albert Einstein, speech to the New History Society, December 14, 1930, reprinted in "Pacifism," *Einstein on Cosmic Religion and Other Opinions and Aphorisms* (1931; repr., Garden City, NY: Dover Publications, 2009), 40.

3. Marianne Williamson, "Day 12," *A Year of Miracles: Daily Devotions and Reflections* (New York: HarperOne, 2013), 39.

Chapter 5: Staying in the Fire

1. "What Is Nonviolent Communication?" PuddleDancer Press, accessed August 31, 2023, nonviolentcommunication.com/wp-content/uploads/2020/09/What-is-NVC-Information.pdf.

2. Dalai Lama, "Compassion Is Nonviolence," *Courier Journal*, May 18, 2016, courier-journal.com/story/opinion/contributors/2016/05/18/comment-dalai-lama-compassion-nonviolence/84553564/.

3. Interview with Kristin Masters, video call, February 17, 2022.

4. Interview with Rachel Pringle, video call, February 24, 2022.

5. David Kessler and Louise Hay, *You Can Heal Your Heart: Finding Peace after a Breakup, Divorce, or Death* (Vista, CA: Hay House Publishing, 2014), 36.

6. Thich Nhat Hanh, *No Death, No Fear: Comforting Wisdom for Life* (New York: Riverhead Books, 2002), 72–73.

Chapter 6: Hiding in Plain Sight

1. Interviews with Dr. Rachel Wurzman, video calls, February 24 and April 25, 2022.
2. Brené Brown, *Rising Strong: How the Ability to Reset Transforms the Way We Live, Love, Parent, and Lead* (New York: Random House, 2015), 32.

Chapter 7: The Karma of It All

1. Lisa Miller, *The Awakened Brain: The New Science of Spirituality and Our Quest for an Inspired Life* (New York: Random House, 2021), 193.
2. Miller, *The Awakened Brain*, 258.

About the Author

Sah D'Simone is a spiritual revolutionary, mystic, artist, and the internationally bestselling author of *Spiritually Sassy: 8 Radical Steps to Activate Your Innate Superpowers*. He is well-known for hosting the top-rated *Spiritually Sassy Show* podcast and *The Big Celebrity Detox* on UK Channel 4 and for creating the Somatic Activated Healing (SAH) Method.

Sah's profound expertise is rooted in a decade of experiential Buddhist practice, his extensive retreat experiences in India and Nepal, and his professional training in contemplative psychotherapy.

As a kinesthetic learner, Sah has danced into trance states since 2015, developing a deep understanding of the body-mind connection. This kinesthetic learning process inspired the formulation of his unique and critically acclaimed SAH Method.

His trauma-informed approach is informed by his grassroots work in orphanages, homeless shelters, and rehab centers in Indonesia, Nepal, India, and the United States. In the near future, Sah will extend his services to Cedars-Sinai Medical Center (the number-two care center in the United States), undergo training in clinical pastoral education, and offer spiritual care to patients in the end-of-life unit. He is also a guest teacher at Columbia University. Sah's remarkable contributions to homeless youth in Venice Beach, California, earned him the CARE award from the city and county of Los Angeles.

Despite his impressive professional journey and achievements, what truly defines Sah is his courage and resilience. From a young age, his life has been marked by battles with depression, anxiety, and addiction, yet his unwavering will to keep living and helping others truly signifies his luminary impact in the fields of spirituality and trauma healing.

About Sounds True

Sounds True was founded in 1985 by Tami Simon with a clear mission: to disseminate spiritual wisdom. Since starting out as a project with one woman and her tape recorder, we have grown into a multimedia publishing company with a catalog of more than 3,000 titles by some of the leading teachers and visionaries of our time and an ever-expanding family of beloved customers from across the world.

In more than three decades of evolution, Sounds True has maintained our focus on our overriding purpose and mission: to wake up the world. We offer books, audio programs, online learning experiences, and in-person events to support your personal growth and awakening and to unlock our greatest human capacities to love and serve.

At SoundsTrue.com you'll find a wealth of resources to enrich your journey, including our weekly *Insights at the Edge* podcast, free downloads, and information about our nonprofit Sounds True Foundation, where we strive to remove financial barriers to the materials we publish through scholarships and donations worldwide.

To learn more, please visit SoundsTrue.com/freegifts or call us toll-free at 800.333.9185.

Together, we can wake up the world.